Breaking Into Broadcasting

Getting a Good Job
In Radio or TV

Breaking Into Broadcasting

Getting a Good Job in Radio or TV-- out front or behind the scenes

by Donn Pearlman

Bonus Books, Chicago

90   89   88   87   86   5   4   3   2   1

Library of Congress Catalog Card Number: 86-70707

International Standard Book Number: 0-933893-16-7

Bonus Books, Inc.
160 East Illinois Street
Chicago, Illinois 60611

Printed in the United States of America

This book is dedicated to my loving, wonderful and very understanding wife, Fran, and son, Russ, who have put up with my frequently long and often irregular hours away from home while I played the unpredictable role of broadcaster.

This book is also dedicated to the next generation of broadcasters: May you be fortunate in finding the jobs you want, and fortunate enough to have a loving, wonderful and very understanding spouse and children who will put up with your own frequently long and often irregular hours away from home.

Contents

Acknowledgments

FOR ALL THOSE nice broadcasters who let me take up their time while I took down their career stories, I say "THANK YOU!" Your experiences certainly will help our next generation of broadcasters.

In addition to those who are quoted by name in this book, I owe considerable gratitude to many others who helped me "behind the scenes."

First, to my Publisher, who patiently waited for about eight years until I finally agreed to write a book for him. I'm glad he kept asking me.

Thanks also to my editor at Bonus Books, Inc., for putting up with me.

Thanks to my employers, especially Gregg Peterson and Carl Dickens, who granted permission for me to write this book. You'll be delighted to know that because I own a personal computer and printer I did not have to continually use the office photocopy machine.

To CBS technician Doug Callihan, who has a great on-the-air voice and could easily slide behind a microphone again, I owe a huge debt. His considerable knowledge of computers and his unselfish sharing of information and software programs saved me literally days of tedious work on this book's index. Doug, my family appreciated the opportunity to see me on those days.

And, to my family, whom I occasionally allowed to venture into my office at home while I worked on the book, I appreciate your considerate understanding, encouragement, and love. I also promise that my office, affectionately known around the house as "The Pit," eventually will be cleaned up.

Maybe after I finish working on the next book. . . .

Donn Pearlman

1

ANYONE CAN GET A JOB IN BROADCASTING—WELL, ALMOST ANYONE....

*"I love broadcasting! I
don't think I'd be here and
put up with all the pressures
if I didn't love it. It's
certainly not the money
that's keeping me here."
—26 year old tv news
assignment editor*

DOES THE POSSIBILITY of reporting the day's events on the tv evening newscast excite you? Have you pictured yourself behind a radio microphone cracking jokes while your delighted listeners are cracking their breakfast eggs? Or, do you dream about an important behind-the-scenes job producing top-rated programs? Or, what about lucratively selling advertising time to eager sponsors who want to broadcast their commercials on your station?

Sounds enticing, heh?

But while you're dreaming of these glamourous jobs why not also envision the possibilities of:

Packing up and moving from city to city every few years as you groom your way up to that tv anchor chair; waking up five or six days a week at 3:30 a.m. to be at the radio station for your morning drive-time show; suddenly looking for employment elsewhere when the previously top-rated program you've been producing is cancelled for reasons entirely beyond your control; or the frustrations of trying to sell advertising time on a radio or tv station while battling cut-throat competitors who promise sponsors virtually anything to prevent them from buying time on your station.

Ah, show business!

Now if you haven't been frightened away yet, then either you giggled all the way through "Night of the Living Dead," or maybe the broadcasting bug really has bitten you and you're willing to spend some time and effort preparing for a challenging and probably rewarding career in the radio and television industry.

(It also could mean that your I.Q. is just a notch lower than the average goldfish, but then you did show significant intelligence when you picked up and opened this book.)

Here is the good news: Almost anybody can get a job in broadcasting. Yes, almost anybody.

No, you can't walk into NBC in New York without any prior experience and say, "Here I am!," and expect the top floor executives to re-name the Evening News in your honor immediately after taking you to a very expensive lunch. They won't even do it after taking you to a rather modestly-priced lunch. They won't even take you to lunch.

Also, having a substantial arrest and conviction record won't be helpful in launching your broadcasting career.

Yet, there are many opportunities to be part of the broadcasting industry. In addition to local radio and television stations, there are cable tv companies, independent production companies, and other industry-related businesses where you can find entry-level jobs.

There is competition for those jobs, but there are plenty of broadcasting job possibilities across the United States for anyone who is determined to enter the business.

According to the Federal Communications Commission, there are 4,718 AM radio stations, 5,106 FM radio stations, and 1,624

UHF and VHF television stations licensed and on the air in the United States. That's a combined total of 11,448 broadcasting outlets that need disc jockeys, newswriters and announcers, teleprompter operators, producers, technicians, sales representatives, secretaries, accountants, community affairs specialists, public relations and promotions directors, program directors, researchers, music librarians, and very importantly—for you—warm bodies to make coffee and answer the telephones as they get on-the-job experience about broadcasting.

In addition to the radio and television stations there are approximately 7,000 cable tv systems operating in the U.S. And, there are thousands of companies that produce or distribute broadcasting hardware and software such as cameras and recorders, and syndicated radio and tv programs.

"But can almost anyone really get a job?," you impatiently ask.

How about these actual examples (details to be found in upcoming chapters): A sportscaster in Chicago is totally blind! A young man with no television experience was able to convince a News Director he would make a good reporter, and he now is enjoying his third promotion in tv journalism. And, a young woman's broadcasting career zoomed in only a decade from her first job inserting commercials on the program log to becoming General Sales Manager of two of the country's biggest radio stations.

On the following pages you will read the comments of these and other broadcasters from across the country, learning how they obtained their first jobs and moved their careers through the industry. The advice of a veteran broadcast technician can help you face your first job in broadcast news; the strategy of someone in television entertainment series production can encourage you in your own search for employment in any field of radio or television.

Carefully read all of the interviews in this book. Although you may only be interested in becoming a disc jockey, for example, the comments of broadcasters employed in other areas of the industry will be very beneficial as you begin your own broadcasting career.

And, even though you may begin your career in one particular area, such as assistant video tape librarian, in a year or two you may easily find job opportunities in other areas of the business; job opportunties that would not have been available to you unless you first had been able to get experience in some entry-level position in another part of the industry.

Although the major networks have been cutting costs by eliminating hundreds of jobs, individual radio and tv stations and cable tv operations still are seeking potential employees.

Broadcasting, as with many industries, is filled with unexpected opportunities. There is some amount of luck involved in being "in the right place at the right time," but once you are booked for that important job interview or actually are selected for employment, your own determination and abilities will dictate whether you remain in that job or quickly move on—either voluntarily or involuntarily.

"Go in it with both eyes open," is the advice to prospective broadcasters offered by Lee Goodman, Professor of Broadcasting and Co-Ordinator of Radio and Television Broadcasting at Purdue University's Hammond, Indiana campus.

"You have to be aggressive. You have to have a personality that wants to move ahead. You've got to have a lot of drive and you've really got to want it bad because it's very competitive. Everybody wants to be a writer or an anchor. It looks like a lot of fun, but it's a lot of work and you can get very bored.

"You have to be creative as well as aggressive, and be ready to put in a lot of hours. And, then you have to accept the fact that when you start the pay is not great.

"I went into broadcasting from the standpoint of business. I was a marketing person, not so much a journalist as someone who liked being in front of people. It didn't seem like work to me. It never bored me to attend mundane Board of Education meetings or Highland, Indiana City Council meetings. I like the excitement. It is always changing, the business is never the same."

Indeed, the industry is always changing. And those changes will provide job opportunities for you.

2

HOW I STARTED IN THE BUSINESS

*"I was paid the prevailing
minimum wage: One dollar
an hour."*

BECAUSE CHICAGO IS my hometown, and my wife's, I made a specific effort to find a job there and remain there. But to be a broadcaster in my own hometown I had to get experience in other markets. (Broadcasters usually refer to cities as "markets." Chicago, being the third largest metropolitan area in the country, is the third largest market.)

My experiences along the way to eventually getting a job in Chicago and building my broadcasting career by staying there demonstrates one kind of determination you eventually may have to face as you build your own career.

Because I only wanted to work in my hometown (and in the words of my family "become a medium fish in a big pond"), I turned down very attractive job offers in New York and California in the past decade. Those were not easy decisions. Broadcasting is a very transient industry. If you remain in a job for a year or two, then move on to another job in another city, colleagues usually do not consider you a "short-timer," or a drifter.

As long as you put in at least a year in one place, and apparently are on a upward career track, your resume could easily list six different jobs in ten years and most potential employers will not care.

Unless, of course, they are seeking someone with stability who will remain with them for more than 12 or 18 months.

But early career jobs often are for short duration. You usually are expected to learn your craft, be a good employee, and then if there are no promotions or challenges available at that station after a year or two, you begin hunting for openings somewhere else. Sometimes you move to another station in that same town or pack up and move to another market.

When your career has advanced past the beginner's stage you may want to consider settling down at a station or in a town you personally enjoy. I know people who are very happy to remain in small or medium sized markets, such as Des Moines. They have no desire at all to "go to the coast," either New York or Los Angeles. As big fish in small ponds they enjoy their surroundings and make comfortable livings with jobs that provide stimulating, daily challenges.

My own stimulating, daily challenges often are literally daily. For several years I have worked six and frequently seven days a week doing both radio and television news in Chicago. With that work schedule and a fair amount of freelance announcing and writing projects I jokingly tell people I see my family on alternate Thursdays.

Monday through Friday I co-anchor the mid-day program segments on "all-news" WBBM-AM. The station, "Newsradio 78," is owned by CBS, Inc. and I have been employed there since June, 1970. In those years I have at times been assigned to every possible on-the-air and reporting shifts—morning drive-time, afternoon drive-time, weekends, and overnights. I've reported on the activities of Presidents and purse snatchers, and have provided many news and feature pieces for the CBS Radio Network.

Before I was given my latest assignment in the 11am-4pm segment I had been working as a reporter primarily covering news and features in Chicago's wide-spread suburbs. The Illinois Associated Press Broadcasters Association named me "Best Reporter" in 1984. The Suburban Press Club and the Chicago Headline Club have also honored me with awards.

My current duties are to write local newscasts, read them on the air, and do a live interview virtually every half hour. The people being interviewed can range from local politicians, eyewitnesses to big fires, to Nobel Prize winners. Sometimes there is adequate preparation time (a half hour before the interview), but usually I am doing a live on-the-air interview with only a few minutes notice.

It is easy to make a fool of yourself with 50,000 watts worth of power to spread your mistakes over the Midwest.

On Saturdays and sometimes Sundays I worked as a general assignment reporter for WBBM-TV, Channel 2, also owned by CBS and conveniently located in the same building as the radio station.

I also produce a short weekend radio feature, "Coin Collectors' Corner," that is a labor of love. I collect coins.

Yes, I'm very fortunate to have these jobs. But I did not just walk into the door at CBS, present my credentials, and immediately be ushered into the studio to boost the already impressive ratings.

I first worked at low-wattage radio stations and a small market tv station with ratings that could only be measured with a micrometer.

My broadcasting career started on the banks of the Kishwaukee River in DeKalb, Illinois. The Kishwaukee, at that location, actually flows backward, from South to North. Fortunately, it was not symbolic of fighting against the stream to get a broadcasting job.

The Kishwaukee flows through the campus of Northern Illinois University. In the fall of 1964 the NIU campus radio station was located near its banks.

Hidden away in the back regions of the NIU "Northern Star"

student newspaper offices was a small low-wattage, non-profit FM radio station, WNIC. Later, when some station elsewhere in the country relinquished the call letters, the station became WNIU.

WNIC was supposed to stand for Northern Illinois College; the school's name prior to attaining University status. However, we had all kinds of other slogans for the call letters. My favorites were: WNIC—We're Never In Control. And, WNIC—Where Noise Is Constant.

A brief article in the "Northern Star" in September, 1964 indicated the radio station was looking for students who wanted to work there, fresh blood. Being a Freshman and not knowing any better, I applied and was accepted for several weeks of non-credit classes an hour or two a week. That's how and where I learned the basics of operating a radio station. Those few weeks of informal classes were invaluable.

I learned how to "run a board" (the control panel switches, dials, and knobs that operate the microphones, tape recorders, cartridge machines, and record turntables). I was taught how to read and fill out a Program Log, how to read the transmitter meters, and I was repeatedly warned that broadcasters are slaves to the clock. If you have only 35 seconds to finish talking before the local station must join the network, you have only 35 seconds; not 37 or even 36.

One other important thing happened during those first weeks of training and learning to pronounce the names of classical music composers. The broadcasting bug bit me pretty hard.

During the Spring semester of 1965 I was made the station's Continuity Director. Now remember, the station was non-commercial. So my job as Continuity Director was to change the Public Service Announcements (PSAs) and Promotional Announcement copy every week. These were index card sized, typewritten pieces of copy that promoted the Red Cross or the Girl Scouts, and urged listeners to tune in for upcoming programs on the station.

It was determined that this easy task of sorting and inserting the PSA and promotional copy into the announcer's files was about five hours' worth of work each week. I was paid the prevailing minimum wage: One dollar an hour.

Since I was working for the state of Illinois I got paid just like all other state employees, at the time, once a month. My checks amounted to only $20 or $25.

But that would buy quite a few golden arches cheeseburgers because they were only 17 cents each in 1965. And, for those lucky enough to have a car on campus, gasoline was only about 25 to 30 cents a gallon.

Still, a dollar an hour was a pretty lousy wage.

So, when I transferred from NIU to the University of Kansas in the Fall of 1965, I immediately looked for better employment opportunities. In November, 1965 I went to work for the local commercial radio station, KLWN-AM and FM. The KLWN was supposed to stand for Kansas. . .Lawrence. But as with virtually any other radio station, the employees there had their own version of what the call letters really meant.

They used to refer to it as "Klown Radio," or "Kansas, Low-Watt Nuisance."

The station was another excellent training laboratory, and by then the minimum wage had jumped to a fantastic $1.25 an hour.

KLWN was located on the vacant Western edge of Lawrence and the station's owner had a few head of cattle in an adjoining field. He used to leave notes scribbled on the program logs: "Water cattle." He wanted the disc jockey on duty to turn on the spigot over the trough. The FCC eventually told him not to write those notes on the program logs as these were official documents. So he started writing them on small pieces of scratch paper and used a paperclip to attach them to the program logs.

(When I lecture now at local high schools or colleges, students often ask me if there is really much difference between working at a 500 watt radio station in Lawrence, Kansas and being at a 50-thousand watt powerhouse in Chicago.

My answer is: Working in Chicago you don't have to worry any more about stepping in it, but you still have to put up with it.)

For a few months I was spinning records on KLWN-FM at night. The AM station was a day-time only station that had to sign off at local sunset. Five or six evenings a week I would play three or four records in a row, tell listeners the time and temperature, and read the few live commercials that were scheduled. I quickly learned how to do my homework while listening for a record to end so I could start up the next one.

Every half hour I was supposed to read the transmitter meters and enter their readings on the transmitter log. This task is about as easy as looking at your car's speedometer and usually is ignored almost as frequently.

I didn't miss too many records coming to an end and soon I was promoted to do the drive-time morning program that was broadcast on both the AM and FM stations (simulcast). And, I got a hefty salary increase: $1.40 an hour.

For this princely sum, I was getting up at about 4:15 in the morning so I could sign on the radio station at 5 a.m. with the Star Spangled Banner immediately followed by a pre-recorded Bible passage reading.

At 9:00 a.m. I would leave the studio, grab a bite to eat, study a little and usually be at my first university class at 10:00 a.m.

I returned home to Chicago in the Summer of 1966 where I was employed as a camp counselor. For two previous summers, I had worked as a counselor at an overnight camp in Wisconsin, but that particular summer I worked at a daycamp. The pay wasn't much better than the radio station, but counselors did get a free lunch everyday and you could go swimming with the kids after you helped with their swimming lessons.

During that summer, I sent a brief audition tape to a radio station in a bigger market, Topeka, Kansas. Surprise, I was hired!

For several months, starting in July, 1966, I was the all-night disc jockey on WREN Radio in Topeka. The pay had increased to a huge $2.00 an hour; considerably above the minimum wage at the time.

However, working all night and trying to keep up with 15 hours of class load quickly took its toll. I submitted a resignation from my job giving two weeks' notice. The station's Program Director and the General Manager did not want to lose me, though. They asked me to at least do weekend newscasts. I agreed and stayed with that very nice station for two years working as a part-time newsman and disc jockey and occasionally working full-time during school vacation periods.

The station was owned by Alf M. Landon, the former Governor of Kansas who was the Republican Party's presidential nominee in 1936.

Governor Landon was very kind to me. A few years after leaving WREN Radio, while working for a tv station in Kansas City, I did a half hour documentary on him.

KTSB-TV, a UHF station, opened in Topeka in 1968. There were already two television stations in town. Channel 13, WIBW, which took its pick of ABC, CBS, and NBC programs, and channel 11, an educational station affiliated with Washburn University.

The UHF station, channel 27, was looking for a news reporter. I applied, and with literally no tv experience except some silly things on camera at a closed circuit University of Kansas station, I got the job. I guess that having worked for two years in the town on a top-rated radio station gave me some "name recognition."

Ironically, I could not really use that name. Instead of using my real name, Donn Pearlman, I had gone under the radio air name of "Donn Mann." It seemed symmetrical and easier to use than my real name. But when I was about to start working at the television station the General Manager insisted that I use my real name.

(In another twist of irony, when I came to Chicago I met and worked very closely with a legendary CBS employee, Donald Mann. His name frequently appeared in various newspaper columns and my mother was always thrilled to see it in print even though it referred to the real Don Mann in Chicago and not the imposter of the plains back in Kansas.)

KTSB-TV was a beautiful station. It was state-of-the-art when it went on the air. Unfortunately, television viewers in Topeka were not accustomed to tuning in ultra high frequency (UHF) stations. The two other local stations, and those whose signals could sometimes be picked up from Kansas City, were very high frequency (VHF) channels 2 through 13.

The management of KTSB-TV had to conduct an education campaign to teach potential viewers how to tune their sets to channel 27. It was not easy to change long-established viewing habits.

I worked at the tv station for only three months. Frankly, I did not like my boss, the News Director.

Now, to get this job, I had to fill out a five page questionnaire that asked things like: "What newspapers and magazines do you read?" (I honestly answered, the Kansas City Star, Newsweek, and MAD.) And, "What is the state of the art of television?" (This was a job application, not a thesis.)

I also had to promise the General Manager that I would stay with the station for at least five years.

All this for a job that paid about 80-bucks a week.

The tv station was an NBC affiliate. Each morning I wrote and read the local, five minute newscasts at 7:25 a.m. and 8:25 a.m. during the "Today Show," headed out the door at 8:30 to cover at least one story in the morning, and then hastily drove to my afternoon classes at KU.

The speed limit on Interstate-70 between Topeka and Lawrence was 80 miles an hour in those days.

On Saturdays, I was the evening news. Literally, I went on the street with a cameraman to gather news, then wrote, produced and delivered the 6 p.m. newscast, including the weather! They did have someone else to do the sports.

As I mentioned, I did not like my boss. Even though the news department had only three people, and could not cover much in town, he did not want us taking anything out of the newspaper, or even quoting a copyright story.

One Saturday the "Wichita Eagle and Beacon" newspaper had some very important, exclusive story about the Governor, and the News Director did not like my writing a story that evening with the words: "According to a copyrighted story in. . . ."

The final straw occurred on Thanksgiving morning of 1968. It was cold. There was a nasty drizzle. And on the way to the tv station on a lonely road between Lawrence and Topeka, Kansas I had a flat tire.

As I fixed the flat at about 6 o'clock on that miserable Thursday morning I vowed to find another job.

When I got home to Lawrence that afternoon, I called a radio station in Kansas City. Earlier that year, at the annual KU Radio-TV-Film Department Spring banquet I sat next to a real, live professional broadcaster from Kansas City. He had been impressed with an audio tape I had made for that evening's entertainment.

So, on that Thanksgiving afternoon I called him at the radio station, WDAF, and asked if there were any job openings.

I was at the right place at the right time. They had an immediate opening for a weekend radio newscaster. Could I come in the next day for an interview?

He did not have to repeat the question.

I had a brief interview with both the News Director and radio station Program Director, wrote and read a brief newscast in a recording studio, and was asked: "If we call you tomorrow, Saturday, can you work the next day, Sunday?"

"Yes, I can," I explained because I worked Saturday at the tv station, but Sunday was my day off. As I worked at the Topeka tv station that Saturday afternoon the Kansas City radio station Program Director called me, said I was hired, and I would work the next two Sundays and then each Saturday and Sunday from then on. I had been hired in a major market.

I immediately tried to find the very nice tv station General Manager who initially hired me so I could give him two weeks' notice. He was not in town that weekend. So I wrote a polite note and slipped it under his office door.

The note tactfully explained that I had trouble working with the News Director. Also, since I was getting married in a few months I needed more money, and therefore, had accepted a job in Kansas City that would pay me for only two days' work a bit more than I was getting for working six days a week in Topeka.

I did sincerely thank him for the opportunity of working at the tv station; I did not want to burn any bridges. That's a lesson you must learn in broadcasting. You never, never know when or where you again will come face-to-face with former colleagues you either detested or only mildly despised.

(In retrospect, I probably should not have even made reference to my problems with the tv News Director in my resignation notice.

In two decades, however, our paths have not yet crossed again. But in this industry you just never know . . . .)

Unfortunately, the General Manager found out about my new job about an hour before he read my note. He originally was from Detroit and he occasionally flew home. That Sunday, when I was on the air for the first time on WDAF radio, the General Manager flew into Kansas City from Detroit, got into his car at the airport parking lot, and as he drove to Topeka on the Kansas Turnpike at 80 MPH he listened to me do the news.

A long hour later, he found my note under the door of his office at the station. It was old news; he already had heard it on the radio.

From late 1968 until June, 1970 I worked in Kansas City, Missouri at WDAF, one of the Taft Broadcasting Company stations. Soon after starting as the weekend newsman on the AM station my duties expanded to include radio and television street reporting a few days during the week. Now and then I anchored a weekend newscast on WDAF-TV, or was the weatherman for the evening news. And when no one else was available I even played the role of weekend sportscaster. I wasn't very good at that, though. I once forgot to give the Raiders football score on a weekend when it should have been one of the biggest sports stories of the day immediately after the Kansas City Chiefs highlights. There were lots of prompt phone calls from irate viewers, including a few from executives of the television station.

It was "a learning experience."

In addition to all these broadcasting chores for the AM station and channel 4 television I also briefly served as the FM station's Public Service Director by recording a weekly, half-hour public service program. In my 18 months I did a little of everything, learning as much as I could about different operations in different departments of the radio and tv stations.

Although I never had to actually perform some of the functions, such as splicing film, learning what can and can not easily be done in different jobs helped me in my own duties. I learned the capabilities and limitations of jobs that directly or indirectly affected my own responsibilities. In smaller stations you can get valuable hands-on experience that may not be available at larger stations.

Kansas City is a very nice community and my wife and I actually were a bit reluctant to leave when I got a job offer from WBBM radio in June, 1970. We still go back to K.C. to visit friends. The area is a fine market for any broadcaster to call home.

I received a job offer from WBBM-AM in Chicago because I was working for the station on a freelance basis as a stringer for news and sports items originating in Kansas City. It was a good time to be a reporter in K.C. The Chiefs won the Super Bowl in January, 1970 and everytime the ailing former President Harry Truman checked into the hospital I picked up a few dollars by telephoning reports to WBBM.

In late April 1970, the Assistant News Director of WBBM called me and said there might soon be a job opening for a Reporter/Anchorman at the all-news station, was I interested? Even though we really liked Kansas City, my wife and I did want to come back to our hometown, Chicago.

Unfortunately, that promised job did not materialize. The Reporter/Anchorman management anticipated they were losing did not get the other job he thought he would be getting. In fact, that guy tried at least a half dozen times to get other jobs either in Chicago or elsewhere in the country, but still is with the radio station.

However, a few months later, in early June, there was another call from WBBM with another job offer. They had an opening for a News Writer. The pay was less than that of a Reporter, but I figured my wife and I would not starve in Chicago; our families were there, and her folks owned a delicatessen.

(I almost did not get that news writer's job. Just as I was getting ready to go to work at WDAF one morning the phone rang and I picked it up in our apartment's kitchen. No one answered when I said Hello. Then I realized, our cat had chewed the phone cord in half.

(Fortunately, the radio station called back a few seconds later and I answered the phone from our extension in the bedroom.)

Ironically, my wife and I had decided just that previous weekend to stay in Kansas City. The radio station ratings were very good, but there had been a huge shake-up on the tv side.

In one week, a newly hired General Manager had fired 19 people! On the Friday afternoon of that catastrophic week, a group of us surviving employees were huddled in a corner when the G.M. came into the newsroom and said: "Your jobs are safe. l will build the station around you...."

I figured it would take at least a year to determine if ratings under the new regime and newscast formats would go up or plunge further down, so my wife, Fran, and I decided we not only would stay in Kansas City, we would get a bigger apartment.

On a Sunday afternoon we put down a $50 deposit on a two bedroom apartment located just 15 minutes from the radio and television stations. It was only $225 a month with a fireplace, parking, swimming pool, and air conditioning included. The next day, Monday, Fran flew to Chicago to buy furniture for the new place.

The very next day, Tuesday, is when WBBM called with the job offer. I located my wife at her folks' house and casually asked: "Did you find some nice furniture?" "Yes," she replied.

"Well," I said, "better find a nice apartment to go with it. We're moving back to Chicago in two weeks."

I started work at WBBM in late June, 1970 as a News Writer. After three days on the job the Assistant News Director told me to carefully watch what the News Producer was doing. I'd be taking over as Morning News Producer on Monday.

I was the Morning News Producer working from 4 a.m. until noon Monday through Friday from late June, 1970 until February, 1971 when a Reporter/Anchor job became available.

I've been on the air at WBBM since then, working in various reporting roles, anchoring every possible mid-day, morning, evening and overnight shift, and even handling some management chores.

In June, 1984 I was asked by WBBM-TV Channel 2 if I could help out by doing some vacation relief reporting duties on the weekends. That temporary job, that was supposed to have ended just after Labor Day, 1984 continued well into 1986.

Interestingly, both the Assistant News Director of WBBM-AM who hired me in June, 1970 and the Assistant News Director of WBBM-TV who hired me in June, 1984 left their respective jobs not long after employing me. The radio Assistant N.D. was ousted in a bitter dispute with new management, the television Assistant N.D. resigned in frustration and now is very happily employed as Managing Editor of a San Francisco tv station's news department after briefly serving as a radio station News Director in Oregon.

I work six and sometimes seven days a week. I am able to maintain that kind of pace because my Monday through Friday radio schedule has been rather stable. Ninety-nine percent of the time I am home for dinner and can spend time with my family. And usually we are all together on Sundays.

With all the extra time on my hands I decided to write this book.

3

OVERWORKED AND UNDERPAID—YOUR FIRST JOB

*"Before you walk in the
door for a job interview,
you should have a very
good idea of what it is you
want to do."*

A LOW-PAYING, entry-level position is an excellent way
of getting paid to learn your career. On-the-job training is standard procedure for beginning broadcasters, even those with advanced college degrees.

Entry-level jobs include an internship while still in school, a
part-time position, or a full-time job in a "beginner's" slot such
as on weekends or at night, or clerical types of positions. As you
will read in the coming chapters, internships are extremely valuable. They get you in the front door and provide you with both
the opportunity to meet and work with people who can later hire
you full-time, and the opportunity to prominently list that internship experience on your job resume.

An internship while you are in school is perhaps the best way to get initial experience in "the real world" as compared to the broadcasting operations at a college or university. The responsibilities and duties of interns greatly vary from one station to another. Some stations limit interns to the roles of "gophers;" you go-fer the coffee, go-fer the teletype wires to fetch the latest news copy, and so on. Other stations may permit the interns to write news or commercial copy, produce programs, do elementary technical work, or even read something on the air.

Whether the duties are limited to being a "gopher" or almost operating the station, the intern is the winner. Interns have the advantage of earning college credits and/or a minimal salary while learning what everyone does in the particular department(s) to which they are assigned during the internship. They are paid for learning how to do their jobs.

Plus, the interns personally meet potentially valuable industry contacts. As you read other chapters in this book, and the comments of other broadcasters, you will see how essential it is to make contacts and also how important it is to avoid making office enemies.

Even after a brief internship, a job hunter can justifiably and proudly headline his or her resume "Worked at NBC/New York...," or something similar to accurately reflect that he or she has "real world" experience in the commercial broadcasting industry.

No matter how much you may have accomplished in school, even being General Manager of the campus radio or television station, when you apply for a broadcasting job in the outside world you probably will find that the primary criteria for hiring you is whether you've had some experience at a "real" station. A two-week internship at a commercial radio or television or a non-commercial station that is not directly affiliated with a school may carry more weight than a high grade point average and three years of experience at the campus stations.

That may not seem fair; however, that is the way it really is with most of the broadcasting industry. There are exceptions, but not many.

With or without previous experience as an intern, you probably will have to knock on many doors to find possible job openings. If you knock on enough doors, one will open for you. In a later chapter there are lists of sources that will point you in the direction of many doors.

To get your first job you probably will have to undergo a ritual called the job interview. It is a rite of passage that, of course, is not limited to the broadcasting industry. Good employment interview skills are needed by hopeful job applicants in virtually every industry.

Sitting down with a Personnel Director or the boss of the department in which you want to work is usually a prerequisite to being hired. In more than two decades of meeting people in broadcasting I've encountered only two people who did not have to conduct an interview with an employer before being hired for their first broadcasting jobs. Their fathers owned the radio stations where they first worked.

Everyone else either knocked on doors searching for employment or they were directly recruited by the employer because their skills and abilities already were known to them. And, in that later case, the young man just happened to be the grandson of a founder of the National Football League and the television station had very close ties to the town's NFL team. Even with those "credentials," this particular employee did have a college degree and some previous experience in another market. He also was skilled enough to not only keep the job once he got it, he since has been promoted several times because of his abilities as a News Producer—not his ability to obtain football game tickets.

And, even with the connections to get him into the front door, he still had a brief interview with the boss before being formally hired.

So, be prepared to be interviewed. It is a selling job. You represent a commodity and you want to convince the potential employer that he or she will benefit by bringing that commodity into the station or office. You have a lot to offer. What you lack in experience you can make up for with an exuberant attitude that demonstrates you are willing to be an excellent employee.

Sure, you want a job in broadcasting, but you have to convince the employer that you are the right person for the available broadcasting job. Remember, the person who is interviewing you for a possible job also once had to look for his or her own first position in broadcasting.

Virtually every week, Karen Nance hears from many people who want jobs in broadcasting. Nance is a Director of Personnel for CBS and her files are filled with applications from hopefuls who either want their first break in the industry or are looking to advance their already-established careers.

She has been with CBS since 1972. Nance got her job in broadcasting because she already was involved for five years with employment and recruitment activities of a health care company.

"People I worked with heard of an opening at a broadcasting Personnel Department and they asked me if I would be interested in working there. I said, 'No, I don't think so. Maybe if it was CBS, I might be interested.' "

"They laughed and said it IS with CBS, so I came in for an interview and about three weeks later they notified me I had it. I worked for about six years as Personnel Manager, and then the Personnel Director left and I took her place.

"It was very easy to transfer the skills I learned at the health care company to the job at CBS Personnel. Plus, I was able to bring some ideas and different viewpoints from my previous company. My predecessor (the Personnel Director) kept saying, 'My gosh, it's like you've been here for ever! How do you know all of this?' "

Karen Nance was able to find another job—and help advance her own career—because of previous job experience. As a Personnel Director who constantly hears from people of all ages and backgrounds who want jobs in broadcasting, she emphasizes the need for some kind of on-the-job experience.

Here is some excellent personal advice from an experienced Personnel Director.

"To get a job in a major market, it will help a great deal if the applicant has some kind of previous broadcasting experience. Many times an internship is helpful, particularly when you're talking about an entry-level job. Some knowledge of broadcasting and some experience are a tremendous help.

"Usually the experience should be in a smaller market (rather than only in college). We're finding that many students get a lot of valuable experiences in internships. Some internships are absolutely incredible in terms of what they offer students. Usually, these internships are available through the schools in either the Junior or Senior year. Some colleges encourage students to go out and seek their own internships and then the school will provide the students with course credits.

"In our industry it is very difficult to get initial job experience. A lot of time the internships will provide you with that entry-level kind of experience and provide an overview of broadcasting operations.

"Many times internships will open the doors for jobs in smaller markets. I've been in touch with students who have grown tremendously over the years. They will go to a small market, having had an internship at a larger station, and land a pretty nice job (in the small market) and then they bounce back to the larger markets and go from there.

"Internships or part-time, entry-level jobs at small stations give you 'bonus points' when you're looking for another job. Many times you can go directly to another station for a full-time job.

"One thing young people must learn about this industry is that you often have to change jobs. A lot of times new employees will go to a station and want to stay there and hope they will go up the ladder there.

"But, unlike a lot of industries, ours is unique from this standpoint: It is better if you go someplace and get your initial training and experience and if something opens up at another station you take it. You move along.

"I think if you look at a lot of the people in our industry who are now Directors and Producers, and you take a look at their careers, they never stayed at the same jobs for a long period of time. They've moved.

"You have to be prepared to move around a lot and get your experience wherever it is offered. If it is in Podunk, go and get some experience. You can always move again.

"Talk to Dan Rather or Tom Brokaw; they'll tell you they started at very small stations, and they just moved along. It pays off in the long run if that is what you want and you are committed to that.

"Before you walk in the door for a job interview, you should have a very good idea of what it is you want to do. Many times when someone is asked 'What are you interested in?,' they will reply: 'Well, I can do anything.'

"That is not a really good response. The interviewer wants to know what your talents are, what skills and abilities you have, and what areas of experience you have. So, you should have some knowledge about what you can do and what you can do well.

"If you're interested in writing but you haven't had a lot of experience, just indicate that 'I'm a very good writer. I have a strong interest in writing and I've done a few things.'

"Many times people feel that if they can get a foot in the door anywhere they can move around. That may or may not be so depending on the size of the station they are in.

"If you are employed in a very large company, and you are working over in the Traffic Department but you really want to be in the News operation, very rarely are the people in News going to know about who is in Traffic and their backgrounds or if they can write.

"On some occasions, I've had people come in for interviews and they brought their mother or father, or a boyfriend or girlfriend. You wonder if the applicant really knows what he or she wants to do, or if their parents otherwise would not believe that they actually went out for a job interview. I always wonder why someone would bring along a parent on an interview.

"Needless to say, it is never a good idea to bring someone else to an interview. It is YOUR interview. It says much more about you if you can conduct the interview on your own. Besides, the more interviews you do, the more comfortable you become about the interview process. It is possible to prepare very well for an interview, and you should prepare.

"And, you don't want to come in loudly chewing gum, eating, or blowing smoke in someone's face. Remember all the things you learned in school about conducting yourself. And, please do not wear such overwhelming fragrances that the interviewer has to leave the room!

"We do get many telephone calls from parents who want to know why their son or daughter who just graduated from college can not find a job. Parents are frustrated having spent a great deal of money educating their children to work in this industry. They do not realize that while there is a lot of turnover for one reason or another, it is very difficult to get entry-level jobs unless you have some experience.

"The parents are the saddest group I have to work with because they've spent a lot of money educating their kids. We have programmed people to think that once you get an education you are guaranteed a job. But, lo and behold, these kids get out of school after their parents have spent a fortune, and there are few jobs to be had in our industry.

"The kids are out looking everyday for a job, from nine to five, and they can't find anything. Usually, they are looking for entry-level jobs and there just aren't that many. They'll call and say, 'I've got a degree in journalism, do you have a job for me?' And, I have to say, 'No, I'm sorry, I don't.' And, you know their hearts just dropped down to their shoes.

"They have no idea where to go next. Now they're looking for anything and it is very sad because there are a lot of young people who never find work in the area in which they studied even though they want to get into broadcasting so desperately. Their parents are frustrated and disappointed, just like their children.

"You have all these schools offering communications courses with several thousands of people graduating, and maybe throughout the country you may have only 200 jobs that are open at the major stations. It makes it very difficult for young people to jump right out of school and into a job, and it takes a lot of patience and persistence.

"Some of the things I recommend these students do is to think about related industries such as production companies, advertising agencies, any type of media company. Again, get back to what it is you really want to do. If it is production, then look at the various production houses. There are a number of them throughout the country. If you are a writer and you want to write for a radio or tv station, then what about writing commercials, what about writing for magazines or newspapers? What about writing for industrial films?

"There are a lot of jobs out there, but you really have to explore related industries, such as cable television.

"And, people tend to think that the broadcasting industry pays a great deal of money for salaries. Because it is a glamour industry people see the numbers of what a Dan Rather reportedly earns, and if he earns six figures then they think everyone else must earn just a little under that. But it is not so.

"Salaries in the broadcasting industry are pretty much in line with most other industries. We are really not that far out of line with places such as IBM (for comparable job categories).

"I urge young people to make as many contacts in the business as they can. Many times those contacts are made socially at parties or business functions. And, you must be up to being a very social person and getting to as many banquets, functions and meetings as you can. Meet as many people as you can and certainly broaden your base of contacts.

"Most of the time the social gatherings are where you will meet the most people and have an opportunity to talk informally and make a slight pitch about your availability. Let them develop some interest in you.

"And, don't burn your bridges. It sometimes is very difficult to avoid conflicts and confrontations with other employees, but avoid it if you can because you never know who you are going to be working for in the future.

"Can you imagine being a News Director and firing someone, then winding up two years later reporting to that same person as your boss? It has happened in this industry."

4

FINE TUNING YOUR FUTURE

*"One of the toughest things
I face in training students is
to make them realize the
fact that they are entering a
career which will take up
the next 40 or 45 years of
their lives."*

IF YOU ARE in school, stay there. A high school diploma is absolutely essential to go anywhere in broadcasting, and at least a few years of college class work are desirable. A college or university degree certainly is beneficial, and may be required for some broadcasting jobs, although an excellent track record of previous work experience can sometimes take the place of a formal higher education degree.

A degree specifically in broadcasting is not always needed. Many successful broadcasters received formal educational training in such areas as business administration, music, theater, journalism, psychology, agriculture, and other academic fields. Broadcasting and communications classes will give you excellent, initial hands-on experience and some perspective on the overall industry, but don't limit your perspective to just radio, television, or film.

As a broadcaster you will need to know much more than just the history of the Federal Communications Commission, the agency that to some extent regulates the nation's broadcasting stations.

Does your college or university broadcasting department have a chapter of Alpha Epsilon Rho? AERho is a national broadcasting society composed of more than 2,000 students and 300 professional members around the country. Each chapter promotes knowledge about the broadcasting industry and its varied activities. Membership in AERho can provide potential job contacts, too.

Alpha Epsilon Rho has chapters at 105 colleges and universities in the United States and encourages students to learn from the experiences of local professionals while earning their school degrees.

The National Executive Secretary of this worthwhile society is Dr. Richard M. Uray, chairman of the broadcasting sequence in the College of Journalism at the University of South Carolina in Columbia, S.C.

"The first question I ask prospective student broadcasters is 'What particular area of broadcasting are you interested in, and why?'," says Dr. Uray.

"If they have no career objectives other than to be a disc jockey for the rest of their lives, then I tell them to go find a job at a station somewhere and let the station train them because that's an area where, comparatively speaking, a college education is of little value. Especially if their career goals are nothing more than just being a jock for the next 40 years.

"If, however, what they're talking about is a long and meaningful career that will provide them opportunities for advancement, for promotions, for moving up into administrative areas then I think they will find that the kind of education they can acquire at a collegiate institution that provides an opportunity for a significant amount of liberal arts education plus a good series of major courses, both theoretical and practical in broadcasting, is the best tool they can have to insure themselves of a significant career.

"They need that liberal arts education because they're going to be called on to have some knowledge about a wide variety of things regardless of where they're working. And, they're going to need that practical training and the theory behind it because if on graduation, for example, they have been trained only to be employees in a Country and Western format station and the only jobs are at Top 40 stations, they're stuck.

"So, they're going to need to get the kind of training that provides them with considerable adaptability. That term, 'adaptability,' is a key word. Most people entering any phase of broadcasting will not be working in that job five years later.

"One of the toughest things I face in training students is to make them realize the fact that they are entering a career which will take up the next 40 or 45 years of their lives, and that they're going to be making many career changes. Their ability to use their intelligence plus the training and education they have acquired—with a high degree of adaptability—will provide them with the best chance for success.

"The liberal arts education, plus a good theoretically and practically oriented broadcasting major sequence, is what they should be looking for.

"Unfortunately, I think there are a number of academic institutions that are far too theory oriented, are far too concerned with course work dealing with theories of communications and theories of this and that. It has to be supported by a strong, practically oriented, lab oriented training program."

For information about Alpha Epsilon Rho—The National Broadcasting Society, write to:

Dr. Richard M. Uray
National Executive Secretary
AERho
College of Journalism
University of South Carolina
Columbia, South Carolina 29208

The society publishes a monthly newsletter for students and professional members and conducts very informative annual conventions. Regional conventions sometimes also are conducted and local chapters hold regular meetings.

When AERho was a national honorary society I was inducted into the organization at the University of Kansas in 1968.

5

BIG JOBS IN SMALL TOWNS VS. SMALL JOBS IN BIG TOWNS

*"Why spend your time
in Peoria?"*

WHILE AT THE University of Kansas I took many broadcasting related classes, but I also studied English literature, public relations and advertising, and even thought about going full-time into psychology. The idea of using a master's degree in psychology to eventually work in marketing or public relations appealed to me.

However, by my senior year I was married and working full-time in Kansas City at a major radio and television facility and I believed that the track record of major market work experience would mean more to potential employers than higher education degrees. At the time, Kansas City was in the top 25 markets. Had I still been working then in a much smaller town, my decision probably would have been different.

That brings up an important decision for you. Do you try to

build a career by starting in a small town, or immediately seek a job in a big broadcasting facility in a big town? Almost everyone interviewed for this book agreed that small station experience is necessary. You will have the opportunities to learn things in a small station that you may never get to learn first hand in a larger operation.

Union regulations may even prohibit you from touching some equipment in large cities, while at small town stations where there are no such restrictions you may be required to be a "one-man band," doing a little of everything. Getting an appreciation for what can and can not be accomplished by broadcasting equipment under certain conditions and time restraints helps you become a better broadcaster.

But not all broadcasters believe you have to start with a small job in a small station. One of those broadcasters is Dale McCarren.

As mentioned earlier, many broadcasters do not have college degrees only in the fields of broadcasting, journalism, communications, speech or business administration. Award-winning and world-traveling broadcast journalist Dale McCarren of WBBM-AM "Newsradio 78" in Chicago also has a degree in psychology.

Early jobs in broadcasting in his home state of Michigan have led to exciting, periodic assignments in the Middle East as he established himself in the major markets of Detroit and Chicago. And, it all began with entry-level jobs in small towns.

"In the town I came from, Saginaw, Michigan, there was a small radio station that offered high school students a chance to come and work at the station. I was one of those students who was able to walk in and say 'WSAM with FM, Saginaw, Michigan.' And, I was hired to work weekends and give the station breaks.

"It was all drama on the radio then. 'Gangbusters' and programs like that from the network.

"When I went to college I needed a job, and the only thing I really knew how to do besides check out groceries or anything like that was to talk on the radio. I'd had a little experience, and so I was able to get a job at the radio station at Michigan State University.

"It was an educational station that played classical music. But being in the front door of that first station in Saginaw, and knowing what control boards looked like and what people did at the radio station helped me.

"The more I did it, the more I liked doing it and the more I became involved in broadcasting even though I was still a business education major. I finished with a business degree from Michigan State but after that I stayed in the broadcasting industry.

"When I was drafted into the military I was with the American Armed Forces Korean Broadcasting Network. The University of Maryland at the time offered a Far East extension program, so I took up psychology. And, all the time I was still broadcasting in Korea.

"So, I've used neither the business major nor the psychology major to get a job, but they've both been helpful in a way."

While many of the people interviewed for this book strongly recommend that those interested in starting a broadcast career begin by looking for work at a small town radio or television station, McCarren offers a different philosophy.

"I've always been of the opinion that if you've got any ability at all, why wait? Why spend your time in Peoria? You might as well bang on the doors in Chicago.

"I know a lot of people who have said: 'I'm going to wait out here (in a small town) until I get enough experience.' Some people get the experience as they go and if they're good, they'll make it with or without experience.

"I've seen lots of people in this business who have no experience, but have the ability. Experience comes. It is like the expression used to describe the presidency, the office makes the man.

"When someone tells you: 'Next you're going to do play-by-play,' and you respond, 'I am?!' You either do it or you go into some other business.

"Basically, I think anyone going into broadcasting should have a Liberal Arts degree. For someone going into news, then a Journalism degree would be great."

6

AD-LIBBING YOUR WAY TO BEING A DISC JOCKEY: BEING CLEVER NINE SECONDS AT A TIME

"Job security is zero."

RADIO IS A part of life in the United States. It is, as the Radio Advertising Bureau describes it, "the go-everywhere medium."

We wake up with the radio for the time, temperature, traffic conditions, and some electronic companionship of music and talk. Radio is with us in cars and trucks, and tiny transistors that accompany joggers, bikers, beach bunnies and ski bums, and those huge "ghetto blasters" that are lugged through the city streets.

Radio keeps us company during the day and goes to bed with us at night. It is available 24 hours a day with just the turn of a knob.

Traditional rock 'n' roll, heavy metal, golden oldies, rhythm 'n' blues, classical, country 'n' western, religious or ethnic, whatever the station format there usually is an announcer to accompany the music. Although "disc jockey" or DJ is the common term to describe the announcer, some refer to the role as "music host."

Before stations used pre-recorded music, when there were live orchestras, bands, and singers, there would be a host or announcer to take listeners through the program.

Arguably, the first major contemporary disc jockey in the United States was Alan Freed who built a phenomenal listenership during the mid 1950's with his nighttime program on WINS radio in New York. A native of Salem, Ohio, he graduated from Ohio State University with a degree in mechanical engineering. In 1957, his live rock 'n' roll stage shows at the Paramount Theater made front page news in "The New York Times" because of the huge crowds he attracted.

Rock music was here to stay and so was the modern disc jockey format of glib chatter and plenty of platter (records).

Today, there are many kinds of music formats. Some stations encourage their music hosts to project their individual personality perhaps with lengthy comments or phone conversations with listeners. Other stations emphasize the music rather than the personality and many disc jockeys are strictly limited in the amount and type of "ad-lib" comments they can make. Some radio formats proclaim "less chatter, more platter," and the disc jockeys literally may have only seconds to say something clever over the few instrumental bars at the start of the latest "hot hits."

In small market stations the disc jockey usually does a little of everything: Playing records, reading news stories that have been ripped from the teletype machine ('rip 'n' read' is the term used to describe that kind of newscast), read the transmitter meters, answer the phones, read the live commercials (and record other commercials before or after the on-the-air DJ shift), maintain the official Program Log by checking off each scheduled segment as it is done and, if the boss demands it, take a broom and sweep the floors.

The salary for this work can range from the current minimum wage, or less, and up.

Being a disc jockey is not very difficult. If you can master the basic motor skills of flipping a few switches on the turntable or tape cartridge machine, closely follow the Program Log, and accurately tell time by looking at a clock, you can be a DJ. The key to being a good DJ is being able to think ahead. To know that when the current record comes to an end you are set up to play the next record or read the scheduled commercial. You have to be in control of the situation.

If you have never before seen a studio control panel, "the board," you may be overwhelmed by something that resembles the cockpit of a DC-10. Some smaller stations have boards that at least resemble a Piper Commanche.

Usually, the switches, knobs, dials, and rheostats are labeled. This switch turns the microphone on and off, this sliding rheostat controls the volume level for the microphone, the next one controls the volume for a tape machine, and so on.

Most radio stations that continually play the same songs over and over during the course of a week make a copy of the record on a tape cartridge that looks like the kind of eight-track cassette you might play in a car or in your home. Usually, however, these "carts" as they are called, contain only one song each, and they have special inaudible cue tones that are "heard" by the cart machine. When the machine "hears" the cue tone, it stops the tape so that after the song plays on the air it is automatically cued up and ready for the next performance an hour or so later.

The more sophisticated the radio station's music format, the more closely the disc jockey must follow the rules. The Program Director and the Music Director may have determined exactly what songs will be broadcast that day or week and perhaps even dictated in what order they will be played. The term "Top 40" radio used to mean that a station was only playing 40 different songs a week, the top 40 songs in the country or in the station's city.

Some formats call for the top two or three songs to be played every hour, around the clock. Other stations may only play certain songs once or twice a day.

The disc jockey's job is to follow the format. If it is your first

DJ job, don't try too hard to come up with zany ad-libs or feel that you have to comment personally about every record, news item or the time and temperature. Instead, learn to segue from one thing into another, make a smooth transition by going from one record to another, or one commercial to another. Learn the basics, then begin to build your on-the-air personality.

Many people who are in different areas of the industry started their broadcasting careers as disc jockeys, or some kind of music host. Perhaps they worked a few hours a week at a school radio station as part of a classroom assignment, or earned money to stay in school by working part-time or full-time at a commercial station in the college town. They did not pursue a life-long career as a DJ, but their experiences at the radio station may have helped them continue in the broadcasting industry.

For example, television game show host Wink Martindale ("Headline Chasers," "Gambit," "Tic-Tac-Dough," etc.) and popular Baltimore tv weatherman Ron Riley both were highly successful disc jockeys earlier in their careers.

Anyone who wants to pursue a career as an on-the-air broadcaster will benefit by having some experience as a DJ. The discipline needed to co-ordinate several things at one time, and do it while talking on the air, comes in handy if you are a talk show host, a radio or tv newscaster or reporter, or even a behind-the-scenes producer or director.

Besides, you then can list on your resume that you worked professionally at a radio station.

On the negative side, in addition to low pay and long hours, especially at smaller stations, on-the-air talent usually is at the complete mercy of the current management. If new management arrives or the station's format suddenly is switched from top 40 music to country and western, there easily also could be a sudden change in disc jockeys.

One of the country's top "jocks" who has survived in a major market for decades by consistently attracting large audiences still realizes his job can quickly vanish due to circumstances beyond his control. This particular DJ started in radio in Idaho and Montana and eventually landed an all-night shift at a big station in a big market. Within a few months he jumped to the afternoon drive-time slot (usually 3pm to 6 or 7pm) at another station in that town.

For nearly 20 years he has worked either afternoon or morning drive-time and has built a large and loyal following of listeners. He presumably also has built a large bank account. But he knows that if the station is sold, or management decides for one reason or another that a change is needed, he again will be looking for work. Even with a labor contract employers can make life miserable if they really want to get rid of an employee who refuses to go along with mandated changes.

Here is what this successful disc jockey candidly tells people who want to get into broadcasting.

"I think the strongest piece of advice I could give to anyone thinking about getting into radio would be the following: Anyone who goes into any branch of the entertainment business—whether it's radio, television or whatever it is—I think is insane. Any time you are in the entertainment business, no matter what branch but particularly in the performing end, job security is ZERO."

Think a minute about your own radio listening habits. Has there been quite a change in disc jockeys on your favorite stations over the last year or two? For various reasons, many disc jockeys come and go, jumping from one city to another. The lure of more money or a station with higher ratings may prompt some jocks to voluntarily move; demands for too much money and poor ratings may prompt management to force some jocks to involuntarily move.

Whatever the reason for a jock moving, it means there is need for someone to fill that job opening. The industry-wide turnover activity creates job opportunities.

So, how do you get your first job as a jock?

If you are a student and your school has a campus radio station then that is the place to start. Sign up.

If you are not a student, see if your community college or a nearby university has broadcasting facilities. You can sign up for the introductory communications course that uses the campus radio station as "lab work."

You can also sign up for courses at private "broadcasting schools" located in some major cities. Some of these schools are very good, but some do little more than take the students' money and offer virtually no job placement assistance. Get references from the school before signing up.

Small market radio stations may have certain days during the year when local civic groups take over many of the chores at the station. If you are a member of the civic group you get a mini course in how to be an announcer.

When you look for work you'll need an audition tape, a brief recording to give potential employers an idea of how you'll sound on their station. Make a tape recording of yourself reading a news story, reading a 60 seconds commercial that you've written, and just chatting for 30 seconds about a popular record, the weather, some interesting news event, or whatever.

Have you ever heard a tape recording of your voice? You probably made a terrible face and thought to yourself, "That's not how I sound!"

When you talk with others you hear yourself from both inside and outside; when you hear a playback of your voice you only hear it coming from outside of your ears. It sounds much higher than what you are used to.

And, if you listen to your tape recorded voice on a tiny speaker it will sound much different than when the tape is played back on better quality recording equipment and through a decent speaker.

Practice reading newspaper stories, magazine articles, record labels, anything. Get used to reading aloud. Get used to hearing your own voice. Get used to talking alone. Often, there will be no one else in the studio when you talk on the radio. Yet, you have to give the feeling that you are talking one-to-one to the audience; not merely reading something into a microphone.

Voice quality is not as important as it was in the earlier days of broadcasting. A rich, melodious voice is a blessing and there are many professional announcers who can make angels sing when they read copy. But today there is more emphasis on voice personality. Does your voice have a high energy level? Even someone announcing an opera in low, quiet tones can have a high energy level.

A typical radio audition tape will contain five to seven minutes worth of material. Two different 30 or 60 seconds commercials, a few minutes' worth of news copy, and then let the prospective employer hear how well you go into and come out of a record. The entire record should not be on the tape, only the first few seconds as you introduce the music, and the final few seconds of the song as you begin talking again. This is called telescoping.

Armed with an audition tape you can contact small market radio stations in or near your community. In small towns there may only be one or two stations in the area. In major markets there are usually many small suburban stations and stations that devote all or part of their broadcasts to programs in other languages such as Spanish, Polish, and German.

These small stations frequently may need part-time staff members to work at night or on weekends. If you are fluent in a foreign language you certainly have a competitive edge in applying for a job at a station that airs programs in that language.

Some small stations will broker time. Instead of selling advertising time in 10, 30, or 60 seconds increments for commercial announcements, the stations will sell a 30 or 60 minutes block of time. The person or company buying that block can broadcast virtually anything they want to air.

Naturally, there will be restrictions on what can be put on the air. For example, there are restrictions on political endorsements, prohibitions on obscene and profane language, and so on. These restrictions are contained in the contract between the radio station and the purchaser of the time blocks.

The purchaser then is free to sell his or her own commercials to be broadcast during those time blocks. The time is "brokered." The radio station may sell a half-hour of time on Saturday afternoon for, say, $200. The announcer purchasing the time block then goes and sells eight minutes of commercial time at $40 a minute for a total income of $320. After paying the radio station $200 for the brokered time, the announcer has made a net profit of $120.

Small stations in small markets, if they broker their time, may sell a one hour time block for only $50. However, advertising rates for commercials may be only a few dollars per minute. (The standard industry joke for these cheap rates is "a dollar a holler.")

It is not easy to build a career this way, but some disc jockeys, especially on ethnic-oriented radio programs, do make a living this way. They purchase time directly from the stations for daily or weekly radio programs and when they are not on the air they personally call on potential advertisers to sponsor the shows.

It is easier to have an employer pay you to work for their station, or get your initial radio experience at a school station.

I knew of a middle aged man, Herb, who worked in a hardware store but really wanted to be a radio announcer. He gently badgered the local radio station owner in a small town to put him on the air. The station set aside an hour late on Saturday nights for him to play a few records and talk about home repair tips.

The first few weeks he did not run his own board. The station had someone there to teach Herb how to cue up the records on the turntables, how to operate the board, and read the Program Log.

By the third week he was almost comfortable operating the board himself. Although he was a terrible announcer when he tried to be a disc jockey, when he started to talk about home repair tips and answer listeners' calls and letters he was fine. With determination and diligence he finally had a radio show, and his employer at the hardware store was delighted to have a "celebrity" on the staff.

I know another person whose hobby was collecting copies of old time radio shows from the "Golden Age of Radio" of the 1930's and 1940's. He persuaded a small suburban radio station that listeners would be delighted to hear tape recordings of such shows as "The Green Hornet," "The Lone Ranger," and "Your Hit Parade."

He has parlayed that first stint a decade ago into six days a week of nostalgia radio broadcasting (and other business-related enterprises).

There truly are many possibilities once you get your first job. Being a disc jockey can be lots of fun and in a major market it also can be very financially rewarding. However, the odds for finding long-term job stability are better in other areas of broadcasting. Not much, but somewhat better.

Twenty-two year old Marc Vernon is preparing for a long-term career in the DJ area of the industry. Out of college less than a year, he already is in his second full-time job in commercial radio broadcasting and is thoughtfully working to eventually become a knowledgeable Program Director.

Vernon works the overnight shift at KFMQ-FM, an album-oriented rock (AOR format) music station in Lincoln, Nebraska. This is a major station in a busy town that is home to both the state capitol and the University of Nebraska. The hours are long, but at the age of only 22, Marc Vernon is steadily building his career. He is actively learning his craft at the studio while studying the trends of the trade by regularly reading industry publications.

"In high school I got involved in the school's radio station and worked there starting my sophomore year. I did everything I could, news and sportscasting, being a DJ and engineering. I enjoyed what I was doing and decided to pursue it in college. My freshman year at the University of Illinois I began working at the student-run, commercial FM radio station, WPGU, and worked there all four years I was in college.

"I was very interested in being an on-air personality. At this point in my life, I'm still an air personality and I eventually want to get involved in programming.

In August, 1985, I got a job at WHMD-FM in Hammond, Louisiana. That's about an hour north of New Orleans and about 45 minutes east of Baton Rouge. That was my first 'real' broadcasting job outside of school.

"I had been sending out audition tapes since the middle of May. About 95 percent of the job leads I found were from the ads in the 'Opportunities' section of Radio & Records (see chapter eighteen).

"I sent a tape and a resume to the Louisiana station and was originally among the final three candidates for this particular job. I missed out getting the job because the station hired someone else. But then about two weeks later the person they hired got a job somewhere else and I was called and asked if I was still interested in being hired.

"My apartment lease back in Champaign, Illinois, was running out and I thought, 'Well, I better take this job and at least I'll have something.' The timing was perfect. I left August first and went to Louisiana where I stayed for seven months before coming to Lincoln.

"I think the size of the market in Hammond, the kind of station WHMD is, all had something to do with me getting hired. They were looking for someone who had commercial broadcasting experience and was a good announcer, but they didn't want anybody who was too experienced—who had been working in a major market and in the business already for 20 years, and who would want $30,000 or $35,000 a year salary.

"They wanted someone they knew they could hire for basically next to nothing. Someone who was young, energetic, and willing to do the things they wanted done.

"On my audition tape, I had telescoped down to about two minutes an hour of one of my shows on WPGU. I took out all the music and (pre-recorded) commercials and left in my voice. There was also a two minute montage of nine different commercials I had produced. The whole tape was only about four minutes long.

"I worked in Hammond just about seven months from August, 1985 to February, 1986. I had originally applied for the job in Lincoln, Nebraska, back in May, 1985. That was one of the first audition tapes I sent out. The Program Director ended up hiring someone else, but the P.D. was one of these rare types who was kind enough to keep me abreast of the employment situation. He first sent me a letter saying, 'I received your tape. I'm interested in you, but I haven't made a decision yet.'

"When he finally hired someone else for the job he sent me another letter saying. 'I've hired someone but keep in touch because radio is a changing business and you never know what is going to happen.'

"I took him at his word and when I got down to Louisiana I sent him a letter saying. 'Hey, I'm here—this is my situation.'

"About two months later I heard that one of the station employees in Lincoln left and I wrote to the Program Director asking if there were any openings yet. He wrote back indicating there were no openings, but he urged me still to keep in touch.

"In December I made some new audition tapes and sent one to Lincoln. About the middle of February the Program Director called to say his overnight DJ was leaving, there would be an opening, and he wanted to know if I were interested.

"Five phone conversations and two weeks later I was on my way to Lincoln.

"It was kind of nice to get a job without having to follow up a classified ad. It was also nice that the Program Director was so very kind and interested in me enough to take the time to pursue keeping in touch with me." Vernon emphasized.

Perhaps another factor in Vernon getting the Nebraska job is that he knew quite a bit about the radio station even before being hired. By regularly reading various trade publications, such as "R&R," "Friday Morning Quarterback," "The Album Network," and "Broadcasting," he knew information about the station's format and some of the personnel there.

Now he knows about the station firsthand.

"I'm working six days a week here in Lincoln. In Louisiana I also worked on a six-days-a-week schedule, although during a seven week stretch I was doing something for the station every day and I didn't have any time off during those seven weeks.

"Right now I'm doing the overnight for six days a week and that has required a little bit of an adjustment for me. I work Midnight to six Sunday and Monday mornings, and then Tuesdays through Friday mornings I work two until six. I also have about an hour of production work to do each day.

"In Louisiana, I would arrive at work at about 3:30 in the afternoon, be on the air from eight until Midnight, and leave shortly after I went off the air. On Saturdays, I was on the air from three until seven, but I arrived at the station about two in the afternoon.

"I enjoy the music. I like AOR format. I like being on the air. I enjoy being an air personality. The next logical step is to move into the position of Music Director, and eventually get a position as Program Director. My ultimate goal is to get into a management position in radio. Right now I'm most interested in being in the music programming end of it.

"When I graduated from college and started looking for a job I told myself, 'I'm willing to go anywhere because I just want to get that first job.' You probably learn the most in your first job. You learn things [mistakes] you don't want to repeat next time.

"You really have to enjoy what you're doing. You really have to love the business, have the drive to work six or seven days a week if you have to. You obviously are not going to make a lot of money to begin with. But eventually, I tell myself, I'll make more and, in the meantime, I like what I'm doing."

7

THE WHO, WHAT, WHERE, WHEN, WHY, AND HOW OF GETTING A JOB IN RADIO NEWS

"I sent out a million resumes and waited around the house for six months until on the same day I had three job offers."

AT MOST RADIO stations putting together a newscast may involve only one or two people. The newscaster rips teletype copy from the United Press International and/or Associated Press news wires, briefly writes up local stories based on articles in that day's local newspaper, and if the station has the budget luxury of having a reporter or two on the staff the newscaster prepares an introduction for the reporter's pre-recorded or live stories.

Increasingly, the clatter of the teletype machines is being replaced by the quiet machine gun pace of dot matrix printers. In the coming years more radio and television stations will convert to computerized newscasting. The information from the wire services will be fed into video display terminals and the news editors, writers and reporters will write and edit their news stories and newscasts on the computer screens, then either read it directly off the screens, or make a ''hard'' copy with the printer.

Still, putting together a radio newscast is a rather simple task compared to the complexity of television news. Even in the largest all-news radio stations of New York, Los Angeles, Chicago, and Philadelphia, only a few people at a time are involved in putting out the product. A technician may be operating the studio control board, a producer rides herd over a half dozen writers and reporters, and the newscaster may or may not be accompanied by a co-anchor to read the stories on the air.

When you count all the newsroom staff members, the technicians, and employees in other departments of even the largest all-news radio stations you won't get much higher than 100 or so. There are scores of news and talk radio stations in the country that survive with only one or two dozen total staff members. (Their local news and talk programs are rather limited, the bulk of the day-long programming comes from network or syndicated sources.)

Radio news provides opportunities for both on-air and off-air jobs. On-air talent must be able to both read a newscast in the studio and hit the streets as a reporter. Versatility is a must today. With increased operating costs station management can not afford the luxury of hiring only news readers or only reporters. The on-air staff members must be able to cover extra alarm fires from the scene as well as smoothly anchor a newscast from the cramped comfort of a studio. Working at a small station, newscasters usually are required to perform both functions.

Working as a disc jockey, acquiring the motor skills and mental dexterity of juggling several tape cartridges while reading something live on the air, is helpful for many newscasters. You may have to run your own board while reading the news. Even if you do not work as a DJ it is necessary to develop the ability to think ahead about what needs to be done next while you are live on the air.

Television producers and directors usually must also cultivate these skills.

Behind the scenes radio news employees are involved in the writing of stories that will be read by someone else—usually without the newscaster getting the time to even glance ahead to what has been written—and are involved in slightly longer range planning and producing of future newscasts and how stories are to be covered by the station.

If you can write simple, declarative sentences you can become a news writer.

That is not as easy it may seem. Listen closely to some of the news writing on local radio stations (and tv stations). With broadcast news the listeners and viewers do not have the ability to go back and re-read an item as with a newspaper. If the news writer has not been clear and concise the result can be confusion.

Most radio stories are very, very short. In a network newscast at the top of the hour some stories may be only two or three sentences in length. That's about 10 or 15 seconds of reading time. Even the reports from correspondents in the field may be only 30 to 60 seconds in length and they probably include 10 to 20 seconds worth of recorded comments from an interviewed newsmaker.

Stories written for local newscasts may also be relatively short, three or four sentences and perhaps a 20 to 30 second "actuality," a tape recorded comment from an eyewitness to a fire or excerpts from the Mayor's ribbon-cutting ceremony at a new shopping center.

If you can master the ability to condense newspaper stories into factual presentations of several neatly typed sentences you will make a favorable impression on potential employers. Add a few informative adjectives and adverbs to the stories, where appropriate, and you can become a valued employee.

Actually, writing radio news stories by re-writing items from local newspapers is not only good practice it is a rehearsal. Because newspaper staffs are so much larger than the radio news departments, the stations must "borrow" stories from the papers.

If you do not have actual examples of stories you've written while working at a station, prepare a dozen writing examples based on newspaper articles to show prospective employers. A well-written, neatly-typed portfolio can help you set up an interview with the News Director or Assistant N.D.

Each station may have its own news copy format as to how the stories appear on each page. A slug (title of the story), the date, writer's name or initials, and time of the newscast are the kinds of things that may appear at the top of the page. Then, skip down a few lines and begin writing the story. Mistakes in typing should be neatly crossed out. Don't bother using any type writer correcting paper or fluid. There just is not time for that under deadline pressures.

The finished story should be legible enough for someone to hit it "cold," read it without problems without ever having glanced at it before starting to read it aloud.

Job applicants who are selected for further screening by the news department probably will take a "writer's test" at the station. In most cases you'll be handed what may appear to be nearly a ton of teletype copy, shown a typewriter and some blank paper, and told to write a five minute newscast based on the teletype news stories. You may be given a time limit of 30 or 60 minutes, and you also may have to incorporate some tape recorded actualities or reports from correspondents in your newscast test.

If you are applying for an on-the-air job, when you've completed writing the newscast you may be taken into a small production studio and asked to read aloud what you've just written.

If you're looking for a job as a newscaster, after you've practiced writing radio news stories based on newspaper articles you should practice reading them aloud into a tape recorder.

Listen to newscasters you've enjoyed on the radio. What do you like about their delivery? How do you compare to their announcing?

Don't COPY someone's style. But listen to it. Develop your own ability to read something aloud with...out...making... it...sound...as...if...you...are...reading...each...word... individually. News reading is best when it sounds both authoritative and almost conversational. The newscaster is telling listeners a story, not proclaiming it from the mountaintop.

After you've gained experience you can begin to build your own distinctive style either based on what you want to do or what your employer may want.

One of the most prominent newscasters in the country is Paul Harvey whose distinctive style attracts tens of millions of radio listeners and television viewers every day. Who helps get all the news for Paul Harvey to read? For his daily broadcasts on ABC Radio it usually is Ron Gorski, an Editor at ABC Radio News in Chicago. Gorski arrives for work at about 5 a.m., but Harvey is already there.

"He comes in (to the newsroom) about an hour before I do, and by the time I get through looking over the wires he has written the basic portion of his (first) show and brings it over to me. I'll go over it and we'll talk about various stories and whether anything needs to be changed.

"He is really a gentleman to work with on a day to day basis. It is a joy to work with him."

Gorski, who briefly left a career in broadcasting to teach English, was so determined to return to the industry that he patiently waited six months until finally getting another job offer. His patience paid off. After six months of no responses, on one day he received three separate job offers.

He has worked in both radio and television and has been with ABC Radio Network News since 1977. "I really didn't think I would be here this long," he laughs. "After doing television work, I thought I would want to go back to it, but now I am not so sure.

"In college, I was a music major, a voice major, and I realized in my sophomore year it would be too hard to make a serious living. I wanted something glamorous, dynamic; so I chose broadcasting.

"I had wanted to be a high school choir director, that was my goal. I still love Baroque and Renaissance music. But I decided that my voice wasn't good enough and I didn't want to work that hard. It is really a tough major. I just didn't have the pipes or the gumption to do it.

"I wanted something interesting that would pay well and be fun to do. And, I chose broadcasting and it really worked out well! It met every expectation.

"My first job was at WIND Radio as a 'call screener' for (radio talk show host) Jack Altman. I did that in the evenings and also worked part-time at school as a cameraman, an audio man, and a technical worker for school classroom productions.

"There were times (when listeners were not responding to Altman's pleas to phone the station) when I would be the caller. On Saturday nights, radio talk shows would either get the 'boozers' or the loneliest people in the world, or no one at all to call. So, sometimes I would be the anonymous caller who would phone in about either puppy dogs or sex. Either of those topics always got the phones ringing.

"I would say I like to torture little puppy dogs, and boom, all these people would call in demanding to save the puppies. Or, I would talk about some bizarre sex story. That would always get the phones ringing. It wasn't hard making up those things.

"The hardest part of the job was trying to determine if a listener's call was legitimate. There probably would be one or two per night that would sneak through. The callers knew they would first have to talk to an assistant producer before being put on the air. And, they knew exactly how to handle it. They would call in, be very polite, cordial, 'Yes, I want to talk about such and such,' and then when they got on the air I would thank God for the seven second tape delay!'' (The ''cuss button'' switch that censors obscene or profane comments.)

"Screening calls was pretty tough. You were 'taken' once or twice a night.

"Jim Benes (a fellow student at college) told me about a summer internship program at WBBM Radio and I went there as a summer writer. After three months I asked if I could stay on. They had some vacancies at the time. CBS was pumping megabucks into Newsradio at the time.

"I worked there for about 15 months and just about went crazy. I couldn't leave my work at the office, I would bring it home and talk about it (stories about racial unrest, political fights, etc.) It was such a part of my life eight hours a day that I couldn't get away from it. It began to consume me.

"I always wanted to teach, so I left the station and taught English and Reading in a junior high school for three years. My wife and I taught there at the same time. We really had a lot of fun, but after a while I wanted to get back in the (broadcasting) business again. Stepping away from it for a few years gave me a better perspective about broadcast news, a better way to handle it."

Patience paid off for Ron Gorski. Patience and determination to re-enter broadcasting.

"After leaving the teaching job I was a school bus driver! I was driving a bus four hours a day and then sitting down and typing up resumes the rest of the day. I wanted to get back into it so bad. Believe me, I love this business.

"I sent out a million resumes and waited around the house for six months until on the same day I had three job offers. I couldn't believe it. I got three phone calls, and my heart was going clunk, clunk, clunk!

"One was from the Media Department of the Chicago Public School system, another was from a television station in Green Bay, Wisconsin. I can't even recall the third one.

"The best offer was from Green Bay. I went up there and got the job at WLUK-TV. My wife and I lived apart for four months. After she finished teaching that semester she came up to Green Bay, but then I had an argument with the News Director and I told my wife: 'I don't think I have long for Green Bay.'

"Two days later I got a phone call from Tom Wolzien, the guy I had replaced in Green Bay as the 10 o'clock news producer. I had never met him in person, but we had spoken several times on the telephone. He was now with KMOX-TV in St. Louis and he offered me a job there. I left Green Bay in two weeks and was producer of the five o'clock news in St. Louis.

"For personal reasons, my wife and I decided to return to Chicago after three years in St. Louis. A person I casually knew who was an Editor at ABC in Chicago told me he was leaving the job, so I interviewed for it, and got it. It really worked out well.

"Actually, though, I didn't start working at ABC until five months after I got the job. Three days before I was supposed to start the new job there was a union strike at ABC. Fortunately, I wasn't yet officially part of ABC or the union, so I was able to stay at my old job in St. Louis on a freelance basis until the strike was over—but that took five months! It's a good thing I didn't burn any bridges at my previous job."

8

IT'S ALMOST NEVER TOO LATE

"I was extremely worried, extremely concerned, that no matter what my audition tape sounded like they might take someone with experience over me."

FEDERAL COMMUNICATIONS COMMISSION rules firmly state that equal employment opportunities will be afforded to all qualified applicants by FCC license and permit holders, the radio and television stations. The FCC general policy states: "...no person shall be discriminated against in employment because of race, color, religion, national origin or sex."

That policy has helped provide previously unavailable opportunities to thousands of minority and female job applicants. Blacks no longer work only at rhythm 'n' blues stations. Women are no longer confined to clerical posts or feature news reporting. Now they not only perform every kind of on-air duty, they represent an increasing number of behind-the-scenes broadcast executives.

Hispanics, Asians, American Indians, and other ethnic groups have gained more access to the media and more jobs in broadcasting. Sure, you may still find some forms of discrimination in broadcasting, just as you can find it in virtually any industry, but equal opportunity is a way of life for most broadcasting executives who must answer to the FCC.

What about age discrimination? Can you be too old to be a broadcaster? Yes and no.

Without getting into detailed specifics about individual company hiring or retirement policies, there can be opportunities for qualified older individuals. If a broadcaster thinks you can help the ratings you may be hired. Look how well Dr. Ruth Westheimer has done with her sex-talk radio and television programs.

Generally, it is best to get into broadcasting at an early age just because most entry-level jobs usually are held by younger people who will be moving up as they gain experience.

Some people know from the start they want to get into broadcasting, but there are those who enter the industry long after they've entered the work force.

———————————

While many broadcasters get their first jobs at commercial radio or television stations while in their late teens or early twenties, Gary Palay didn't begin working at a commercial station until nearly a decade after leaving college. Although he majored in broadcasting at Southern Illinois University, after leaving school he pursued a career in a family-owned retail clothing business.

Palay emphasizes that broadcasting is something he has wanted to do virtually all of his life: "I knew I wanted to do this when I was three years old and held up a fork and talked into it like a microphone!"

When Palay finally decided to launch a career with his "first love," broadcasting, he was 29 years old. He had no broadcasting experience outside his radio and.tv work at SIU, but he had considerable determination and some luck. Palay's very first job is providing him with both on-the-air and management duties. He is News and Sports Director of KLZY-FM and KPOW-AM in Powell, Wyoming.

The "Big Horn Basin" listening area is only about 35,000 population, but Palay says the salary at his current job is better than in Billings, Montana about 90 miles away where the population is about 150,000.

"This is my first job in broadcasting. I took the first job that was offered to me because I thought it might be difficult to get back into the business after more than eight years away from it (at the family clothing store). When the station said they wanted me, I came running.

"I found them through an advertisement in 'Broadcasting' (magazine). I made an audition tape through some facilities at Northwestern University. I had a friend who let me use a radio studio there. After eight years, of course, I didn't have a tape, so I had to make one.

"After I sent out the tape, the station called and I took the job. I wasn't going to be particular about the area (of the country) or the job itself just to get back into radio, if I could.

"The stations at SIU were a tremendous opportunity. We worked both television and radio. Besides news and sports we had a half hour newscast every night with news, weather and sports. And, I had a half-hour program on the college-run station, and did play-by-play of football, basketball, and baseball. Between the practical experience and the classroom instruction, I felt I was at one of the better broadcasting schools in the country.

"But I was extremely worried, extremely concerned, that no matter what my audition tape sounded like they might take someone with experience over me. But luckily, after hearing the tape and talking with me on the telephone, they offered me the job. It was really that quick.

"Again, I didn't want to be in a position to get a couple of different job offers because I thought it was more important just to get back in.

"I'm thrilled to be back in radio, but now (after 18 months at the stations in Wyoming) I'm actively trying to find another sports position and I'm sending out tapes to stations in other parts of the country. That is my first love. Hopefully, my next job will be full-time sports.

"It has been somewhat frustrating trying to find a station in a medium or major market that is hiring a full-time sportscaster. There are not many opportunities to send audition tapes without just fanning them throughout the country. Yet, it certainly helps that I have the on-the-air and management experience here in Wyoming. I would have no chance (in a larger market) if I were coming in cold with no experience outside college.

"If I wanted to move to a news job there would be no problem, I would have plenty of offers. But there just are not a lot of sports jobs listed that I know of. It becomes tremendously frustrating trying to find the job openings."

Typical of many broadcasting jobs, Palay puts in long hours.

"I'm in my office at 5:30 in the morning and I leave at 5:30 at night. I'm the only newsman. I do news on the hour on the AM from seven until five with three, 15 minute news blocks during the day at seven, twelve and five. The other newscasts are two minute updates on the hour.

"The AM station is Country Music. The FM is Adult Contemporary format. We have two morning drive-time newscasts at about 6:50 and 7:50, about four minutes each, covering a quick look nationally and locally and a feature item. And, there is an afternoon newscast on the FM at about 4:50.

"So, I do three newscasts on the FM, all the rest are on the AM. And then I do two news blocks that are four to five minutes in length on Saturday on the AM. In addition, there are meetings to cover because we are a one-person news department now."

9

THE WHO, WHAT, WHERE, WHEN, WHY, AND HOW OF GETTING A JOB IN TELEVISION NEWS

"The job interview in Green Bay took six or seven hours. It was grueling."

WHILE RADIO IS the workhorse of broadcast journalism, television news is the prancing pony. It gets most of the attention and newsmakers know it. Politicians and publicists used to arrange news conferences for the convenience of the newspapers to meet their deadlines. Now events are staged to coincide with the early and late evening tv newscasts.

The powerful camera lens has its advantages and disadvantages for broadcasters. Television news generally pays considerably more than radio news jobs (and the average radio news writers and announcers in many markets usually earn more than newspaper reporters).

You can broadcast the news daily for years on radio and after a while some people will recognize your name. But show up on television only a few times and you may not be able to unobtrusively walk into a drug store without being noticed. Television newscasters are personalities. For many viewers, the anchors and reporters ARE the news.

Promotional campaigns for local tv newscasts often depict the newscast anchors dashing to the scene of a breaking story. Indeed, in small and medium sized markets, the anchor probably does put in a long day covering one or more stories, editing the video tape, and then sitting behind the anchor desk for the 10 p.m. or 11 p.m. newscast. The anchor may also be the station's News Director, too.

But in some larger markets the anchor may never hit the streets for a story because his or her contract firmly prevents it. They are to be anchors only, no getting those neatly combed hairdos ruffled by the wind at the scene of a story.

Former NBC-TV "Today" show newscaster Floyd Kalber, now a top-rated early evening newscaster at WLS-TV, Chicago, is quoted by the *Chicago Sun-Times* as saying: "This garbage about anchors 'on the go' working the news on the street is just that—a lot of garbage. It's all just promotion to show the hard-working newsman with his sleeves rolled up and his tie askew and all that crap."

When you begin appearing regularly on television you may lose all your privacy. I jokingly tell people that you can't beat your wife and kids in public anymore. (Please don't write to me about domestic abuse. I am very much aware of the nationwide problems. The joke is only to make a point about lack of privacy.)

When you go shopping on your day off if you don't comb your hair or shave, or if you just wear a sloppy ensemble of comfortable, torn jeans and paint-splattered shirt, viewers seeing you on the street or in the stores may wonder about your on-air credibility. Unless, of course, you are the station's "life style" reporter and that's the way you sometimes appear on camera. . . .

As glamorous as television news may appear it is tinsel glamour, fleeting fame accompanied by long hours and newsroom doors that keep revolving. If you work in television news you learn not to make too many long-range dinner reservations.

Yes, there are many, many opportunities for very rapid advancement and huge salaries. Major market anchors earn six-figure salaries. Executive Producers of these newscasts can command salaries of $50,000 to $100,000. But, the pace of the business is very fast and very competitive.

A television news broadcaster, either on camera or behind the scenes, should be well-read, open-minded, not easily flustered and very flexible about working conditions. You should be prepared for extreme highs of joy when you win an award or the ratings are good, and be prepared to pack up and move to a far-away town a year later when a new Boss takes over the station and wants to repay a career debt to someone by giving your job to another straight-toothed, expensively dressed "90 day wonder" who doesn't know the difference between Washington, D.C. and Washington Irving.

Surely, you have noticed the "musical chairs" of anchor people and reporters on the newscasts of your own local tv stations. As with radio disc jockeys, and to some extent radio newscasters, there is a high turnover rate in the television news industry. People move from station to station, city to city, in search of better jobs. Or, if they have involuntarily left their last employer, they're just searching for jobs, period.

A radio reporter may have only one person to appease when putting together a story, the News Director. The reporter may not even have to deal directly with the N.D. or even a technician when writing, editing and finally recording the story.

However, television news is a team effort. The reporter works with a Producer (who is keeping close contact with the Executive Producer), a Writer, mini-cam Camera Operator, Sound Box Operator (to record the sound portion of the tape), and finally the Video Tape Editor. (In smaller stations, the reporter may do virtually everything including operating the camera while conducting an interview.)

Then, after the story is edited on tape there is the anchor who will read the introduction to the story while getting his camera cues from the Floor Director while the Director in the control room and other technical staff members are literally putting the program on the airwaves.

You sometimes wonder how it all comes together!

Sometimes it doesn't. We've all seen glitches and foul-ups during newscasts. When things go wrong on radio you can make a face or point any finger you wish at someone and the audience never knows how you've reacted.

There are many ways to get an entry-level job in a television newsroom. Again, a student internship directly in the news department is desirable. However, jobs in other departments of the station can lead to the newsroom if you let the News Director or Assistant N.D. know you are interested in filling the next vacancy.

Being able to write simple, declarative sentences—a key to success in radio news writing—is only one aspect of being able to write good television news copy. The words to be read by the newscaster usually must accompany some kind of "visual," a photograph, a map, some film or video tape. The visual elements will tell part of the story, the words being read by the newscaster supplement the pictures.

A major criticism of how tv news executives determine what stories they will put on the air is directly related to the medium's dependence on visual elements. Some Producers don't say, "What happened in the news today;" instead they ask staff members, "What do we have pictures of?"

And whether it is radio, tv, or print journalism, the basics do not change: Accuracy, fairness, and balance. Unfortunately, I've encountered too many reporters, print as well as electronic media, who never let facts get in the way of a good story.

Television news copy has many more markings on it than radio copy. In addition to the slug (story title), writer's initials, date and time of newscast, there will be video cues indicated on the left side of the page. Cues for the Director to signal a "super" (superimposing a name or address on the screen at a specific time during the story to identify a person being interviewed or the location of a news event), which studio camera may be used and even which anchor person is to read the copy.

Individual writers will be assigned by the Producer to write specific stories for specific newscasts. The Producer may indicate what direction the story should take; start the story with the fact that an investigation into yesterday's fire is continuing rather than leading with "A fire has destroyed a high- rise building...."

Watch how the major tv network correspondents use visual elements along with written copy to tell the stories. Major and medium market television stations usually also make extensive use of video tape, charts, graphs and other visual stimuli to not only tell the stories but create a flashy package that will attract and retain viewers.

(In case you forgot, the more people in the radio and tv audience, the more money the advertising sales departments can charge for commercials. The more high-cost commercials on the air, the more revenue the stations generate. The more revenue coming in, the more likely the station will continue to keep all the employees on the payroll and perhaps even hire more staff members.)

It is difficult to walk in the door of most tv stations with absolutely no previous experience and expect to be hired as a newswriter, producer, or reporter. There are exceptions as you will read a bit later. Radio newswriting experience can be beneficial, but some tv executives have a low opinion of radio and for some reason do not think radio broadcasters can make the quantum leap to television.

Yet, a background in radio provides experience in writing tightly, watching the clock, and understanding the basics of broadcast journalism.

You may find it easier to get a job in a small or medium market tv station if you have some radio experience, but usually employers are looking for previous tv work experience. And, that experience should be at a "real" television facility, not the student station on campus.

The scores of private broadcasting schools across the country offer television courses as well as radio. As mentioned earlier, some of these schools provide excellent training, but others will leave you hundreds of dollars poorer and with no job prospects.

Get references of satisfied graduates from the school before signing up.

Prepare a small portfolio of a half dozen or so tv writing samples demonstrating your ability to write hard news stories (fires, car wrecks, political bickering) and feature stories. As with getting a job in radio news, tv news applicants may also be requested to take a "writer's test" to show how well they can prepare stories under deadline pressure.

Being determined to get a television news job may be the most important aspect of actually getting one—determination to keep looking for a potential employer to convince that you are just the person needed for his or her newsroom. And then after you've landed that job, you begin preparing for moving up.

Often, the fastest way to move up the career ladder is to pack up and move to another city every few years rather than wait for a promotion at your current place of employment. In a period of about six years, 29 year old Howard Epstein of St. Louis has moved from a college internship in Chicago to full-time television jobs in Green Bay, Wisconsin, Dayton, Ohio and now to Columbus, Ohio.

With a little help from a teacher, and by exhibiting his own excellent judgement and attitude in an exhausting series of personal interviews, Epstein was able to get a job in television news even though he had no previous commercial television experience. Today, he is a reporter with WTVN-TV in Columbus, a station that is part of the successful Taft Broadcasting chain.

"My first, full-time job was at WBAY-TV in Green Bay. I started there in March, 1979 soon after I graduated from Northwestern University. A Professor in the Journalism School helped me land that job because the Assistant News Director there was a former student of his.

"The station was looking for a reporter. I was able to get the job without even an audition tape to show them my work. The only thing I had available was an audio tape, but no prior television experience. The photograph I sent them was from my wedding.

"I was surprised I was able to get a job that easily. I had heard all the horror stories about every year they graduate enough journalism school students around the country to replace everyone now working in the business. I thought this was going to be a tough nut to crack.

"I had worked as an intern at a Chicago radio station (WBBM-AM) trying to get some ground-floor experience while I was still in school. I thought that might help me.

"The job interview in Green Bay took six or seven hours. It was grueling. They wanted to figure out what kind of a character I was. I didn't have anything to really show them what I could do although I was able to give them some writing samples. So, I was kind of surprised they would hire me that easily.

"But it worked out very well for me. I would credit it to the fact that I went to a good school, the connection I had with the Journalism Professor, and the experience I was able to get while working in school. The internship also carried some weight; the fact that I had worked in the business to some degree at a quality operation. That also gave me a feel of what it was like in the business and so I came in with realistic expectations. That helped as well.

"I worked in Chicago as an intern for about six months, and then I was hired on as a Desk Assistant and worked as a D.A. for about two years.

"The job interview at WBAY took just about all day. I met many people from their staff from the General Manager on down. The News Director, the Assistant News Director, the Producer, the prime news Anchor, and so on. They were asking how I would handle certain situations. They would present different scenarios and see how I would respond.

"I think it was just an attempt for them to try and get to know me and let me get to know the members of their staff. They finally concluded afterward that even though I lacked experience in television, they felt that I had the basic tools; the ability to write and the ability to tell stories that I could handle myself. That's why they gave me the opportunity.

"I was in Green Bay for about two and a half years. I worked doing a little bit of everything.

"When I first started, they were changing over from film to video tape, and I learned how to shoot film—a little bit, not very well. Then I learned to shoot a video tape camera. I was a reporter and we used to go out in tandem. I would shoot another reporter's story and then he would shoot mine. We did that for a while until they eventually hired full-time photographers.

"My primary reponsibility was to be a reporter, but I did some producing, worked as a part-time Assignment Editor to fill in, and I also anchored the news a little bit on the weekends.

"I did a little of everything while I was there. It was a great experience because I learned and got a chance to do everything and find out what the business is like. What it is like behind the camera, behind the scenes, as well as in front of it.

"That has been a valuable experience. Now where I'm working when a photographer points a camera in a certain direction I get a clear image of what he is shooting and I know the limitations of the video tape camera and I know what I can expect to see when we get back to the station. There are no surprises any more.

"When I left Green Bay, I went to Dayton, Ohio, WKEF-TV. There were no real prior contacts to getting that job. It was just contacts I had made on my own. I had made a couple of trips through Ohio—Cincinnati and Dayton, and Indianapolis, Indiana—making contact with News Directors and letting people see my work (on video tape).

"I had talked with the News Director of WKEF-TV several times and in October, 1981 he called me because there was an opening at the station and he offered me the job. We had talked a couple of times earlier and hit it off pretty well. It had taken me a good nine months to finally land something, but banging on the doors and showing my video tape did it.

"I came to Columbus in June, 1984. The News Director here had called a co-worker of mine in Dayton and told him there was an opening and asked if he was interested in applying for it. The guy at the time was not interested in it, but said he had a co-worker who might be, so he turned the phone over to me.

"I talked with the News Director and he invited me up for an interview. A couple of days later I went there with an audition tape and it was a much shorter interview (than for the Green Bay job); only about two hours or so with the News Director and one of the Producers. About a week later, the News Director offered me the job in Columbus.

"I'm a general assignment reporter basically working from 2 p.m. or 2:30 in the afternoon until about 11:00 at night. I do live shots for both the early and late news, general assignment reporting.

"I'm glad that I did what I could to learn about the business while I was in school by working at the college stations and also getting an internship. The internship taught me that this is not a nine-to-five, Monday-through-Friday business. You have to work weekends and holidays.

"Where I'm working now there are many Ohio State University graduates who are trying to get jobs in Columbus. They think they can do the work, but then they find out they really don't have all the experience they need to work at a commercial radio or television station."

The importance of an internship at a radio or television station, cable system, or any broadcasting related company can not be overemphasized. The internship provides direct one-on-one contact with the company executives who make the final decisions on who will be hired.

Even if you do not get your first job directly as a result of an internship, it may help you get your second or third position.

Twenty-five year old Vickie Burns has been a professional broadcaster for only a few years, but she has steadily moved ahead in her television news career. Just four years out of college, Burns produces the early and late evening weekend newscasts at a major market, network-owned television station, and is Assistant Producer of the station's weekday five o'clock newscasts.

Her weekend chores actually begin during the week when she looks ahead, with the station's News Planning Department, to possible Saturday and Sunday events to be covered. On the weekends themselves, her duties begin from the time she awakens in the morning and calls the station to talk with the Overnight Assignment Editor and then the Daytime Assignment Editor.

She usually arrives at the television station by 10:00 in the morning and does not leave until about 10:45 that evening; even later if the 10 p.m. newscast has been delayed because of other programming.

Despite the tremendous pressures of setting up from scratch and riding herd over four separate, half-hour newscasts each weekend, she does not panic easily. Burns has the ability to plan ahead and anticipate what quick changes may be needed to make the live broadcast run smoothly. Because she worked at the station as an intern, she has an excellent grasp of the duties, possibilities, and limitations of many other jobs that affect her responsibilities, such as graphics, directing, reporting, and technical operations.

"I started at WBBM-TV in Chicago in January, 1981 as an intern. I was very lucky, I had a really good internship that gave me quite a bit of responsibility and I was allowed to learn a lot about the workings of WBBM. My timing must have been just great because three weeks after the intership ended I interviewed for a job in the newsroom which was a big change for me, moving me more in the direction I wanted to be in.

"The internship was for a public affairs show and it was a different side of the business altogether. I really had always wanted to get into news and I just got lucky when I called the newsroom and said the usual: 'I'm a student, I'm looking.' And they said, 'Well, why don't you come in and talk to us, we may have something for you.'

"So, I didn't have to wait around and do a lot of searching before I actually found a job. I was still a student when I did the internship and it was a full-time position. My title was Intern, but my role was more along the lines of a Production Assistant for the show. I actually was involved in the production, the meetings to decide which segments would be included on the show, deciding which guests would appear, a lot of responsibility I thought for an Intern.

"The internship definitely led to my next job, not directly because they were two different areas of the business, but indirectly in that I worked in the (same) building and I got a chance to meet and get to know the people who eventually would hire me.

"Originally I was a pre-law student and I did not switch my major to communications until the first semester of my Junior year. I did it because I had taken a few classes (in communications) just for the fun of it, and I loved it.

"After my internship, my first job in the newsroom was working as an assistant in the News Film Library. Basically, I would find tape (of previously broadcast stories) for re-use in updated reporters' stories, I logged newscasts. It was a very lowly, clerical kind of job.

"For someone who is just getting into the business, I would tell them to take anything that you can get. Get to know everyone you can. Don't worry if you don't know right away what you want to do because it takes time, and there are so many more jobs in the business that you don't know about until you actually get in the door. Don't feel discouraged if you think that you're in an entry-level position for too long, because it's never too long; you're always gaining more experience.

"If it's not direct experience, it's certainly life experience."

Connie Buscemi works with Vickie Burns. At the age of 26, she too has been in broadcasting for four years and started her career with an internship. She literally went through a blizzard to get her first full-time television job.

Buscemi now helps plan how stories will be covered at WBBM-TV in Chicago. On weekends, she is in charge of the Assignment Desk and dispatches reporters and crews where they are needed and initially checks out details on breaking stories such as fires, crashes, or news tips from viewers. It is an important job that requires fast thinking and the ability to work well with all kinds of people, often under stressful situations. Buscemi performs the the tasks very well.

During the week, in addition to her duties inside the station, she occasionally becomes a Field Producer and goes with a crew and sometimes a reporter to the scene of a story. Buscemi will co-ordinate coverage on the scene and, if there is no reporter, she will conduct interviews with the newsmakers.

She wants to use these experiences to eventually move into higher news management positions, such as Producer of the newscasts.

Interestingly, as she was just starting her broadcasting career, Buscemi was rather demanding about her first job. There were certain television stations where she wanted to work, and not others.

"When I started here I was an intern for (television reporter) Harry Porterfield. I produced the feature series 'Someone You Should Know.' It was my senior year in college and the Chairman of the Communications Department at Columbia College came up to me and told me it was about time that I got an internship, what would I like to do?

"I said that I wanted to work in News and I told him there were specific stations where I wanted to work. (Laughing) Well, I figured I had nothing to lose, so what the hell!

"Channel 2 was one of the stations where I wanted to work. So the Department Chairman set up an appointment for me, and I did several interviews with several different departments at the station. Harry and I hit it off and that's how it started.

"I already did have a job at the College and a full load of classes, and then I got the internship at the station at the same time. Why I didn't collapse, I don't know.

"My initial duties were to screen potential stories for the 'Someone You Should Know' feature series. I would set up the interviews, actually do preliminary interviews, accompany the reporters and sometimes act as Field Producer, and sit in on the editing process. Overall, I would give my opinion when it was and when it was not asked for.

"I had that job for about five or six months and when the internship was over I expressed an interest to stay at the station. That was well received.

"I had made friends with the News Department Librarian and when her assistant was transferred to another department the News Director asked her who she would like as a replacement. She immediately suggested me and the News Director said that was fine.

"He then gave me a call and I came down here (to the station) in a blizzard to get the job.

"I was able to use a connection from my first job to get my second job here.

"I like broadcasting. I love it as a matter of fact. I don't think I'd be here and put up with all the pressures if I didn't like it. It's certainly not the money that's keeping me here.

"I'd like to advance, maybe be a full-time Field Producer then go on to maybe Executive Producer or Weekday Assignment Manager. Something where you're not locked away in an office, but you've always got your hands in the nitty gritty out there with everybody else.

"For those just getting into the business, I would say show a lot of determination because some people don't think that it really shows, but it does. Prove that you are willing to do anything, and I think you must be willing to give a lot of yourself to really make it.

"There are times when you think it is not worth it and people are not paying attention, but it pays off. You think people aren't watching, but they know exactly how much you've put into it, how hard you've worked, and how much it means to you.

"If you want to succeed, you will."

10

PROLIFIC AND PRUDENT PRODUCERS

*"I can train almost anybody
to be a television producer
if they've got some basic
smarts."*

ALTHOUGH VIEWERS MAY only notice Dan Rather sitting alone at the anchor desk, the CBS Evening News certainly is a team effort. A team that literally is spread around the world.

For two years one of the broadcast journalists in charge of giving that team effort a daily direction and shaping the network's half-hour broadcasts was Lane Venardos, former Executive Producer of the CBS Evening News and now Executive Producer of the CBS News special events unit. Viewers watch the newscast in the early evening (or late afternoon depending on where in the country it is being seen), but the day would begin many hours earlier for Venardos and his staff.

"My day began at home in the morning listening to the six o'clock radio newscast. I was usually in the car on the way to work by 6:45 or 7:00, and I have a phone in the car so I would have a conference call in the car on the way to work. That saves lots of time.

"The broadcast is on the air at 7:30 p.m. (Eastern time) and I would leave the office about eight."

With typically wry humor, Venardos explains how his love of broadcasting began in college and tells about his first jobs at small radio stations.

"While attending the University of Illinois at Champaign, I chanced upon the campus radio station, WPGU, which was the undoing of my University of Illinois college career but launched me inexorably on the path in broadcasting which has led to this checkered career that now stretches behind me like so many rusted hulks in the desert.

"My first job there turned out to be the carrier-current- radio-station anchorman on the once-a-week Wednesday Noon broadcast. The radio station had a non-paid staff of several hundred students, each of whom had sort of one little thing a week to do, although some had a couple of things a week.

"That blossomed into a job at the radio station in my hometown where I went back to recover from the University of Illinois. That was in Alton, Illinois at WOKZ: Tall tower, full power, first, fast and factual—always first when seconds count—1570 on your AM dial!

"I worked four hours a week on the FM station whose wattage was barely sufficient to reach the base of the tower, I sometimes thought.

"From there I went to work in St. Louis while simultaneously working in beautiful Alton, Illinois and then on to WBBM in Chicago.

"At the U of I, I had started off thinking I wanted to be an electrical engineer which was incorrect, and I ended up majoring in business administration with a minor in Spanish.

"I have a daughter who is now attending Ithaca College and who wants very much to be a part of this crazy dance. She says she wants to be a network television producer or maybe a reporter.

"I tell people (who want to get into this business) that experience still is the biggest arbiter of the kind of people that I hire on the CBS Evening News, but that the kind of experience one gains in a college where there is some hands-on experience possibilities seems to be preferable. And, further, that I think the courses one should take in college, from my perspective, should lean heavily on English, Political Science, History, Civics, and not necessarily toward Broadcast curricula or Communications.

"I can train almost anybody to be a television producer if they've got some basic smarts. What I can't do is make them write (well). Writing skills are paramount around here toward being a successful television producer."

Writing skills led to the first broadcasting job for Steve Friedman, the very successful Executive Producer of the NBC-TV "Today" show. Each morning an estimated six million Americans wake up to the eye-opening interviews of Bryant Gumble and Jane Pauley, the weather forecasts of Willard Scott and the newscasts of John Palmer.

"Today" is on the air for two hours each weekday, but Friedman usually works more than 12 hours a day to produce these programs.

As a teenager, Friedman enjoyed sleeping past ten o'clock on weekends. Now he is at the office by 5:30 each morning. "It is the worst match ever, but they weren't going to move the show to Noon," he joked.

As Executive Producer he oversees scores of writers, technicians, clerical staff members, and other "Today" show employees, and he juggles millions of dollars in programming and scheduling decisions that can take the show—and viewers—almost anywhere in the world. Despite all these stressful responsibilities, Friedman admits, "My hardest job is getting up in the morning. Once I do that the rest of the day is easy!"

And, despite the early arrival at the office, he usually does not head for home until about six in the evening.

While attending the University of Illinois Friedman worked at the student-operated station WILL-TV and majored in radio and tv. His first job after college lasted only three months. He was among many people hired to convert WBBM-AM in Chicago into an all-news station in 1968.

"They hired all these people to get them on the air, and then after they were on the air, they figured they could lay off 20 of us," he recalled.

As a newswriter, Friedman worked virtually every shift at the radio station during those three months of employment.

"The best shift I had was three in the afternoon until Midnight. The worst was eleven at night until seven in the morning.

"When the radio job ended in Chicago I decided I wanted to get into television so I went to Los Angeles. I got a job at KNBC-TV as a newswriter. I didn't know anybody out there. I just went.

"It was a lot different in the industry then. In 1968 and 1969 all the 'smart' people in Journalism School wanted to work on newspapers. And now all the 'smart' people want to work on tv. So, the field was more open back then. Also, television newscasts were expanding.

"The reason I got a job at KNBC-TV is because they were going from one hour of local news daily to two hours and they needed people to help them do it.

"I stayed in Los Angeles until 1979. From 1969 until 1977 I worked at KNBC-TV as a newswriter, then weekend producer, and then I was doing special projects for ratings periods (so-called 'sweeps' pieces). I produced the five o'clock news program from 1975 to 1977. Then I got a job with the NBC Network in Los Angeles doing features for the 'Today' show.

"Eventually, I was asked to come to New York to produce the show. I did that for a year and they made me Executive Producer. My feature pieces were so brilliant that I guess that's why they gave me the job," he said with a laugh.

As Executive Producer, Friedman determines exactly what will go on the air, when it will go on, how long the segment will last, and who will work on it. "I also make sure the commercials get on the air," he added.

"I start work each morning at 5:30 and I'm there until six each night. At nine o'clock in the morning, when the day's broadcast has ended, we begin working on the next day's program as well as other future broadcasts.

"One of the secrets is to hire smart people and let them do their jobs and then take the credit for what they do. There are two ways to go: One is to surround yourself with dopes and you become indispensable. That's one way of running things. Another way is to do what I do—hire the best people you can find and let them do their job, then you take credit for what they do.

"I think that's the best way to go. Now if any of them are smart enough to knock you off [from your job], great, terrific. But I think if you surround yourself with stupid people, then you're stupid.

"For anyone thinking about getting into the industry I would suggest that you spend your 20's doing as much as you can in the business, spend your 30's making your mark in the business, and spend your 40's living off what you did in your 20's and 30's. By the time you're 50 get out.

"It is a young person's game. The hours, the pressures. If you really want to make it in this business, you have to develop a specific skill over time. Unionize, specialize, etc. You can't just say, 'I want to be in tv.' You have to have some idea of where you want to go, what you want to do. Whether you want to be a writer, a producer, a camera operator, whether you want to be on the air, or whatever.

"And, as far as being on the air is concerned, if you look at your tapes and you're not the best thing you ever saw, get off. The chances of making it are slim."

11

MAKING THE TEAM
AS A SPORTSCASTER

*"Football season is the
hardest part of the year."*

THERE ARE BASICALLY three different kinds of jobs involved in sportscasting. Reading the scores and sports stories as part of job in the radio studio or on the tv news studio set (and perhaps doing sports-related interview programs on radio or tv), doing play-by-play announcing at the actual sports events, and the often complex and exhausting work of producing sports programs.

Good play-by-play broadcasting involves time consuming preparation by the announcer and the behind-the-scenes staff. Even the sportscaster who broadcasts the local high school football or basketball games on a small town radio station certainly has done his or her homework before the game, looking over results of previous games, players' histories, and so on.

Doing this kind of play-by-play on a small market or suburban radio station is a fine way to break into the business. The station may not have a full-time sportscaster, the sports scores may be included in the newscasts by the station's lone newscaster or read by the disc jockeys when they do the news. Yet, the station may be able to successfully encourage advertisers to sponsor broadcasts of local high school athletic contests.

Surely, the sons or daughters of local merchants are on the teams and those merchants' advertising dollars would pay for the broadcasts.

Approaching a small market radio station with that concept can lead to a part-time play-by-play job. I know a small town elementary school principal who has been doing it for years and when he started he had absolutely no broadcasting experience except doing public address announcements in his school every morning.

Practice doing play-by-play while watching a game on television. Use the daily newspaper's sports page for studying information about the players in the game, their jersey numbers, their statistics, some side-bar information about comments they've made to reports. If you have video cassette recorder (VCR) with a separate audio recording feature why not record your play-by-play comments as you record the video of the game on the screen.

Play it back at the end of the game and listen critically to yourself. Were you able to keep up with the action (ice hockey and basketball can be difficult)? Did you call the plays accurately?

After you've practiced calling several complete games you can record your next sportscast on an audio cassette or tape reel and you've made your first audition tape.

Most of the private broadcasting schools around the country provide instruction in sportscasting and play-by-play. Remember, not all these schools actually provide job placement assistance after you've paid your tuition and gone through their classes. Get references from satisfied graduates before enrolling.

Student stations at high schools and colleges are excellent training facilities for prospective sportscasters. The local high school station may also use adults from the community for sportscasting chores. Check it out. Enrolling for an announcing class at a local college or university can also provide initial experience in putting together sportscasts and doing play-by-play broadcasts.

Full-time sportscasting jobs usually are limited to medium and large-sized markets. Only stations in bigger towns may be able to afford the luxury of a full-time sportscaster. (Read the comments of news and sportscaster Gary Palay in chapter eight.) You must be willing to move to another part of the country if that is where the job being offered to you is located.

Behind-the-scenes sports jobs, aside from technical positions such as operating a camera or other video and audio equipment, involve planning pre-game, half-time, and post-game programs and production of the actual sports events.

A sports producer can make or break the sportscast. The preparation before the sportscast or sports event is crucial to the success of the broadcast. Lining up interviews, packaging short special reports for use before and during the game, and being ready to provide informative statistics during the game itself are some of the tasks.

For regular television newscasts, a sports producer or assistant producer may watch games in progress and isolate specific plays during the game for video tape highlights on the station's newscast later. When there are several simultaneous games the work gets complicated trying to keep track of the action and make sure all the different taped highlights are ready for the newscast.

On the following pages you will read the comments of three sports broadcasters. Each has different jobs, different responsibilities and functions. But they all have two things in common: They love sports, and they work very long hours.

This book contains many examples of people determined to get jobs in broadcasting by overcoming some obstacles to achieve their goals. But what if the obstacle is not one of age or lack of experience? What if it is a physical disability?

Bob Greenberg is a radio sportscaster whose voice is heard in both St. Louis and Chicago. He does color commentary on various play-by-play broadcasts, locker room interviews, and regularly scheduled sportscasts on WBEZ-FM in Chicago and via telphone hook-up to KMOX-AM in St. Louis.

Most of the listeners, however, may not know that Bob Greenberg is blind.

Greenberg uses a Braille-like stopwatch to time his interviews and reports, and a "talking" wrist watch to literally tell him the time. Sportscasting colleagues marvel at his ability to retain information he has heard and recall at will numerous statistics, incidents, and sports anecdotes.

They also have expressed amazement at his ability to do other "impossible" things such as getting interviews with baseball player Reggie Jackson and National Hockey League star Wayne Gretzky at times when both were usually declining to make comments to the media.

"There are a lot of people who might go out of their way to talk with me because I can't see, but I don't solicit that because I think that is being unfair to other sports people. I don't want anybody to feel sorry for me because I'm handicapped, but at the same time I want to be able to do my job," Greenberg explained.

His interview for this book was conducted by mobile phone. Greenberg was riding on a Chicago Transit Authority commuter train to the Northwestern University campus in the suburb of Evanston to cover an N.U. basketball game. He carries a portable cellular telephone that permits him to call in his reports and keep in contact with the radio stations.

"You have to get a good education to be a good broadcaster. I think going to a college is very important, more important than going to a 'broadcasting school.' I think many of those kinds of instructional schools are rip-offs, although there are some decent ones.

"If you want to get into broadcasting you have to be willing to start in a small town. There is no doubt that you have to be willing to make a lot of sacrifices. That means working long hours.

"It is four o'clock in the afternoon now and I've already worked an eight hour day, but I'm on my way now to do a Northwestern-DePaul game this evening. The week before, I also covered sports events in the evenings on three days as well as worked eight hour days at the station.

"You have to keep a lot of crazy hours and when you first start out in broadcasting you've got to be willing to work for low pay. If you happen to be handicapped, it is even tougher to get a job. Depending on what the person wants to do in broadcasting, it would be a good idea to have a background in a little bit of everything.

"I actually started out in broadcasting when I was 13 years old. When I was 12, I went down to a radio station to meet someone I had always listened to, Stan Dale, and he introduced me to Herb Graham, an announcer for radio and television commercials. Herb became my announcing teacher for about a year.

"A lot of people had a lot of confidence in me, confidence that I could do it. I used to take apart and put back together old radios.

"When I was 13 I started on the air as a time broker, buying my own time on the air and then selling commercials to pay for it on a small suburban station. I started out as a rock and roll disc jockey and gradually got interested in sports. I did sports interviews on that program for ten years on that station.

"In college, at the University of Illinois in Urbana, I worked as News and Sports Director for WPGU (the U. of I. student station). Then after college I had a couple of stints at small stations in Evanston and Highland Park (Chicago suburbs), and I even worked for a candidate for the U.S. Senate back in 1972. That was very interesting; I learned a lot about politics.

"Then I worked as a narrator and tape editor for a correspondence school for about three years and did a lot of freelance sports work for ABC Radio before going to work for WBEZ. And, now I also do sports reports out of Chicago about the Cubs, White Sox, Bears, Bulls, Blackhawks and the Sting Soccer games for KMOX in St. Louis.

"Some people might say that working at a high school or college station will help get you a job, but that is not necessarily true. Most broadcasters don't really consider that as 'experience.' You have to really prove yourself and the best way to do that is put together a good audition tape. You have to know how to run a studio production board, and have to know how to ad-lib.

"I think you have to be prepared for anything in that first job, and be prepared for long hours. Take advantage of every opportunity," Greenberg emphasizes.

One of the busiest broadcasters I've met in my more than two decades in a very hectic industry is Eric Mann. As an Associate Producer for CBS Sports he is likely to visit three or four different cities in a week, then be back in New York by Saturday morning to begin putting together special pre-game, half-time, and post-game features for the weekend Brent Musburger tv programs such as "The NFL Today."

Actually, Associate Producer is only one of Mann's titles. At the age of 27 he also is an Associate Director, Feature Producer and Feature Director.

Mann's late father, Donald Mann, was nationally known throughout CBS and the broadcasting industry as the most successful radio sales representative in the country. Although his father may have been able to set up job interviews for him, it was Eric Mann's own hard work, determination and creative talents that helped move him through the ranks at CBS Sports.

"Basically, it was a matter of being in the right spot at the right time. I graduated from Northwestern University and got my Master's degree there and I always had been interested in news. My father knew several people around CBS News, and when I walked in there to do a job interview in New York they mentioned to me that there were possible openings at the Sports Division and at CBS Cable.

"I had always loved sports. I covered sports in college and enjoyed going to every sports event, and even have a huge collection of sports memorabilia—it was right up my alley.

"So I set up some interviews there and it was, just like I said, being at the right place at the right time.

"My first job was Broadcast Associate (B.A.) which is an entry level job. You're responsible for a lot of arrangements like hotels, air fares, and you co-ordinate getting video for features, promotional teases, things like that. And, you line up the graphics that are needed for the broadcast, the Chyron or Vidifont units (the typewriter-like devices that are used to produce on-screen lettering for identifying people or events during a broadcast).

"You program all that information. You have to be ready for any kind of late-breaking situation when you're doing that. You have to be ready for whatever can happen during a game. You have to know the game inside and out. It's your judgement while your talking to the Director and Producer during the game. Many things are automatic, like baseball batting averages, downs and yardage in football.

"I spent two years doing that and for me it was a natural progression from being a B.A. to move up to Associate Producer and Associate Director."

Aside from traveling across the country almost every week, Eric Mann frequently goes overseas to cover sports events.

"Yeah, I've been in some strange places! I went to Belfast, Northern Ireland to cover a boxing match. I've been all over Europe and to South America for the Pan-American Games. You do get to travel an awful lot and visit a lot of different, interesting places; places which I certainly wouldn't have been in had I not been in this job.

"It is definitely not a 40 hour a week job. Definitely not. You work a lot of hours.

"As an Associate Producer, for example, for football games I'm usually helping to script and sit in on the editing of many promotional teases. I do a lot of that. And, then during the show I help the Producer roll on the commercials.

"Football season is the hardest part of the year. My work week starts on Sunday evening when the day's games have ended and goes through the next Sunday evening. We're non-stop.

"Audiences think there is only one game going on at a time, the game they're watching. But on a lot of Sundays we actually have eight games being broadcast almost simultaneously. It's a lot of work. 'The NFL Today' is more than just what the audience is seeing. We're on the air from 12:30 in the afternoon until 7 at night.

"During the NFL season we start at the studio at 8 in the morning and finish usually at 8 in the evening, but Saturday nights we are up very late getting everything edited and ready for the next day's show. It takes a while. Often Saturday is a longer day than Sunday, we sometimes are up into the wee hours just getting everything ready for Sunday's show. It doesn't just happen by itself!,'' Mann said with a laugh.

What job could be better than that of a network sportscaster? You get to travel, you get to see the big games, and you get paid for it, too!

But there is a tremendous amount of time and energy needed to properly prepare for coverage of the sports events. The football season activities of former New York Giants star Pat Summerall demonstrate the strenuous schedules of network sportscasters and commentators.

During an on-the-air interview with me on WBBM-AM, Summerall explained that his preparation for play-by-play coverage of a Sunday NFL game actually begins the week before at the conclusion of the previous Sunday's game.

At his home in Florida, Summerall views copies of official NFL films of the teams he will be covering. These are the same films that the NFL uses to monitor the performances of the referees and other on-field officials.

Summerall studies these films for most of the week to familiarize himself with the players he'll be covering that coming Sunday. "I want to know the players so well that if they didn't wear numbers on their jerseys I could still identify them," he explained.

He travels to the town of the home team and on Fridays he meets with members of the network's broadcast crew to view the latest game films of the two football teams they will be covering on Sunday. Following the viewing, they discuss what they've just watched and analyze the offense and defense strategies of the teams and players.

"Saturday is a day for personally meeting with the players and the coaches and watching the practice sessions of the teams. Saturday evening we review what we've learned and talk about what we want to emphasize on the next day's broadcast. John Madden (former NFL coach and also a CBS sports broadcaster) and I spend a lot of time talking about what we think each team has to do in order to defeat the other.

"We just don't walk into the broadcast booth and it all spews out, and then we leave and have fun. It's a job, but it's a job that I enjoy very much," Summerall stated.

His sports coverage duties are not just limited to professional football. "Gosh, I've done everything for CBS from dog shows to barrel-jumping," he said with a smile.

As soon as the NFL season ends, Summerall follows the professional golf circuit. He also covers tennis matches for the network.

"That takes care of 51 weekends out of the 52."

12

GETTING TECHNICAL —
BROADCAST ENGINEERING

*"Be a 'gopher' and
do everything."*

A GROWING AREA of potential broadcasting employ-
ment is the technical field. Surprisingly, though, most of the job
opportunities may not be at the radio and television stations. The
growth apparently will be in the independent production companies
that supply programming to the stations and to cable operations,
and there will be growth in editing houses, the companies that edit
and mix the audio and video tapes to produce a finished product.
Independent companies that produce radio and television commercials are also potential employers for those seeking entry-level jobs.

There has been an explosion in advanced technology in broadcasting the past 20 years. Video tape virtually has replaced all use
of film in the tv newsrooms. The portable cameras ("mini-cams")
are lighter and more versatile. The high quality reproduction audio

tape recorders used by most radio stations easily fit in a brief case or purse, or are even as small as a pack of king-sized cigarettes.

Because of the advanced technology of electronic news gathering (commonly called E.N.G.) many stations no longer want to retain as many technicians on staff. In large cities where unions used to require a three member field crew for shooting a news story—camera operator, sound operator, and lighting technician—there now are only two-member crews. On a limited basis some major market stations are using "one-man bands" where one technician does it all; lights, camera and sound recording with a hand-held beta cassette recorder unit.

In smaller markets, reporters often do double duty, both conducting interviews and shooting the video tape.

Where major market radio stations would have an engineer on duty to run the control board for a disc jockey or talk show host, the announcer now does "combo," talks on the air and operates the board. Combo is standard operating procedure in medium and small markets. The only full-time technician at the radio station may be the Chief Engineer who is responsible for maintenance of the equipment and to make sure the transmitter is sending out the signals on the correct frequency.

Therefore, many radio and tv stations are not replacing engineers and technicians as they retire or change jobs. Through this attrition, and in some cases outright layoffs, it appears that engineering jobs at many stations are fading out, they are few and getting fewer.

The good news is that many of these same stations are hiring part-time or per-diem technicians to operate the studio cameras and mini-cams, to run the control boards, and edit video tape. The positions may be listed as "V.R.," vacation relief, and may last for anywhere from several weeks to several months. Often, skilled V.R. employees eventually may be placed on staff full-time if there are vacancies to be filled.

In larger cities, some technicians make their livings by working at different stations during the year. They will work at the NBC station for several months, then when that job is over, they jump to the ABC station for a few months, and so on.

Freelance jobs are also available with the independent stations (not affiliated or owned by one of the major networks) and with cable operations, such as CNN.

Being a mini-cam crewmember can mean putting in very long hours outside in bitter cold or sweltering hot weather, and working for weeks without a day off. Just like a reporter's job, field crews usually do not know where their jobs will take them. They can be away from the station for the entire day, or even sent out of town for days at a time.

During the 1985 Middle East airline hijacking incidents some technicians and reporters were away from their homes for weeks at a time, moving from Greece to Lebanon to Italy and finally to West Germany as the hijacking-related events unfolded.

The "easiest" technical job is working with sound. Setting up studio microphones and running the control board are virtually the same for radio and television. A mini-cam sound engineer watches the volume control meter on "the box," the video tape recorder unit, and either lets the reporter hold the "stick" microphone or the technician uses a hand-held boom or shotgun microphone to pick up the audio.

Often, entry-level technical jobs begin with working the sound systems.

A steady hand and a good eye for composition are needed to be a good camera operator. In the studio, the Director will tell the camera operator how to frame the shot. In the field, the mini-cam operator uses his or her own judgment unless the reporter wants a specific shot for the story.

Other technical jobs at television stations include studio lighting, switching (changing the camera shots at the direction of the Director), maintenance and repair of equipment, editing video tape (another area where a good eye for composition and transition can make or break a story) and dubbing (making copies of programs or commercials for later broadcast).

There also are grapics operators, the technicians who run the equipment that superimposes letters, numbers and other visuals on the screen. Usually video font operators sit in front of typewriter keyboards which hammer out the desired lettering and electronically store it in the computer memory until the Director calls for its use.

That is a simplified run down of the kinds of engineering jobs found in most radio and tv operations. Companies that manufacture broadcasting hardware, of course, also hire technicians to develop new products and systems.

When looking for a job, technicians who specialize in camera work put together short video cassette audition tapes showing a half dozen or so stories they've shot. Video tape editors will also provide audition cassettes demonstrating their skills at the editing console.

I know several tape editors who do not just watch the tv series "Miami Vice," they study it to learn tips about editing sequences together.

It may be difficult to get "real world" experience in some areas of broadcast engineering without actually working at a major commercial television station. However, once you get into the station you either will have the opportunity to learn on your own about the different functions or the employer will be switching you around to different tasks so you can be a jack-of-all-technical trades.

As the next interviewee strongly recommends, the more you know about technical operations the better potential employee you will become.

All of the interviews in this book are with men and women who are either just starting their broadcasting careers or are well-advanced in the industry. All except this next interview.

After more than 35 years with NBC-TV, Arnold Margolis retired on Dec. 31, 1985. During his final years with the Proud Peacock network, Margolis was a Senior Video Engineer and he wrote a 260 page "Video Control Engineer" manual that all NBC technicians now study and use. He also personally trained many of those employees about new technology video equipment.

Margolis has seen many technological changes in his three and a half decades at the RCA Building in New York. But some things don't change, such as the need for new employees to be eager to learn, and to have some prior experience before they even walk in the door.

"When I started with NBC I was a Maintenance Engineer (fixing broken equipment and doing routine adjustments to prevent equipment from not properly functioning.) I just walked in and applied for it in 1950 when there was no competition for jobs. I had gone to school and taken engineering and actually was a television repairman in 1950 before I came to NBC. And, they were hungry for people like that. Nobody knew about television!

"So, that was one of my first jobs when I came in; I was fixing television sets in the offices of some of the executives.

"There was a big wave of hiring that started at the end of 1949 and it continued until about 1954 when they hired between 500 and 600 engineers. Then they stopped hiring for about ten years. Then, when the technology improved they expanded further and started hiring in large numbers again. I am part of the older crowd that is begining to retire now.

"I have found that nobody coming from school is worth anything when they come into NBC. They are useless, because none of the schools teach what is required. They teach generalities and when people come to work at a place like ours, even as a temporary employee for vacation relief work, they are useless until somebody takes them in hand and starts to train them the way we require them to work.

"You have to have a general understanding of what is going on at the station so you don't walk around wide-eyed. It is almost like giving new employees a guided tour. 'Oh, this is a studio!' or, 'This is where Saturday Night Live comes from.' Regrettably, this is how our new employees all look.

"They have to familiarize themselves with the facts of life beforehand. It makes it very, very difficult to handle them until they begin to catch on. They don't know the technology because no one is teaching it to them because the technology isn't out there for them to practice on (at most schools).

"The suggestion I have for any newcomers is to get out of New York or Chicago or Los Angeles and go to a small town, go to some tea kettle station somewhere. Be a 'gopher' and do everything. The station will be grateful because they don't have lots of other staff members there. Learn the craft at that level.

"Then, when you come into the bigger cities, you'll at least have some experience under your belt and from there moving up to network standards is not that traumatic a shock. You can be useful to your employer far more rapidly. You will have learned the words, something of the terminology, the lingo, the technology, of what goes on, and it won't be that strange to you later.

"If you get hired as a temporary, a Vacation Relief (V.R.) engineer, you'll be given most of the menial jobs—laying down cables and wires, microphone boom pushing, and so on. If you have a flair for it and can demonstrate skills, maybe you'll be turned loose on a camera on some of the more simple (studio) shows.

"And, even though the kids don't realize it's happening, people will watch them like a hawk to see what they're doing. The older employees around them will watch them surreptitiously to see how they're doing. The recommendations (on who to retain for full-time employment) will be made to the boss by the old hands. The feedback comes back that way.

"Then, when the Fall comes around and the Summer vacation period is over, they will lay off most of the V.R. people, but a small handful may be held on to help replace those who have retired.

"In network television operations, I see the number of available jobs holding at a steady, stable rate. But outside, in the production houses and editing houses, I see it increasing. The future job opportunities will not only be at a network or a network owned and operated (O & O) station in a major market.

"Look at the credits for some of the shows now on the air. You get many of the independent companies doing most of the specials today that are shot on location (out of the studios). That's not done by network people. These are often done by independent production outfits with mobile units and per-diem crews."

13

OTHER POSITIONS – OTHER POSSIBILITIES

"I'd say that you have to believe in yourself and don't be afraid to show that."

THE PUBLIC OFTEN does not realize there are many behind-the-scenes broadcasting jobs. Radio and television stations, and to varying degrees cable systems and other broadcast related businesses, hire marketing researchers, public relations and promotions specialists, advertising time sales representatives, editorial writers, community and public affairs specialists, and staff members who prepare the official Program Logs and the live and recorded commercials.

Middle and upper management positions also include Program Director, News Director, Production Director, Operations Manager or Station Manager, Sales Manager (and sub categories such as Retail Sales Manager), Business Administrator or Financial Department Director, and Chief Engineer (with other sub categories at larger stations).

Entry-level jobs can be found in such areas as community affairs, promotions and publicity, continuity, and depending on other work experience of the applicant, editorials, marketing, research, and sales.

The Community Affairs Department works as a liaison between the radio or television station and the local community. The department usually handles public service announcements (P.S.A.s) and will keep records about how the station is serving the "interest, convenience and necessity" of the community to which it is licensed. There frequently is contact with community leaders, luncheon speeches, and perhaps even conducting tours of the station.

The Promotions Department co-ordinates the promotional activities of the station. The department is a liaison between Sales, Programming, and the General Manager's departments. If the station will set up a remote broadcast at the County Fair the Promotions Department will handle publicity before, during and after the event, and will be involved in special events during "the remote," such as having a banner with the station's call letters, handing out to the public bumper stickers with the call letters, giving away prizes to listeners who attend the event.

The Promotions Department will also be involved in on-the-air promotional announcements that advise listeners about upcoming programs on the station.

Previous broadcasting experience is not really needed to work in the Promotions and Publicity Departments, just a strong desire to work hard, work with other people, and learn.

The Continuity and Traffic Departments are responsible for making sure the commericials are "in house" ready for broadcast and that they are correctly placed on the Program Log, the written schedule of what is to be broadcast and at what time.

These are jobs that require considerable attention to detail, and involve frequent last-minute changes as commercial copy arrives late, doesn't arrive at all, or needs to be changed. Although this is not a clerical job as such good typing skills are essential.

Many larger radio and tv stations have computerized their Continuity and Traffic Departments and that makes life easier. But there are still those last minute changes when the station's sales representatives rush through the door just before quitting time and insist that two dozen commercials be inserted into the next morning's log.

And computers have not yet replaced common sense. Broadcast commercial copy is meant to be read aloud. Seeing something in print may be quite a bit different than reading it aloud. For example, there was a pancake house that had a Gold Rush era theme and the copywriter who wrote the radio spot (commercial) for the restaurant wanted to convey that image to the audience.

Unfortunately, one of the first times the commercial was read live on the air, the announcer went into a hysterical fit of laughter. The copy stated: "(The restaurant's name) pancakes are so good, they'd make any prospector drop his nuggets!"

The Traffic Director also must not place competing sponsors near each other on the Progam Log. There must be at least a few minutes' separation between, for example, two competing beer brands, clothing stores, or automobile dealerships.

You also have to be careful about the juxtaposition of some non-competing sponsors. Early in my broadcasting career, at WREN in Topeka, the Traffic Department innocently placed a funeral home commercial immediately adjacent to a Pepsi Cola spot. During the 1960's Pepsi frequently used the theme: "Come alive! Come alive! You're in the Pepsi generation!"

The disc jockey on duty dutifully followed the Program Log by first playing the pre-recorded, somber spot for the funeral home, then, as it ended, he promptly hit the tape cartridge button for the Pepsi commercial that began with the musical invitation to "come alive, come alive!"

The funeral home owner was not amused and threatened to yank his commercials from the air. He was assured the incident would not be repeated. The Traffic Department carefully made sure the funeral home commercials were placed away from any possibly interfering spots.

It went well for about a week until the disc jockey segued directly from the funeral home spot to the start of a Trini Lopez record that began with the lyrics, "Got along without ya before I met ya, gonna get along without ya now...."

I think the DJ may have done it on purpose.

The Editorial Director is responsible for coming up with suggestioned topics for editorials, the researching of material for and the writing of the editorials. Sometimes the Editorial Director will be the radio or tv stations' editorial spokesperson and deliver the editorials on the air.

The Editorial Director also must seek out opposing viewpoints to the station's editorial positions and get those opposing views on the air for rebuttals.

Because of the competitive nature of broadcasting—there are just so many potential advertising dollars available and all the stations are battling each other for a share of them—station Sales Departments always look for a competitive edge. Everyone may get the same ratings books, but each station will try to interperet the ratings to their own advantage.

Radio station "A" may have the highest total number of listeners between 6 a.m. and midnight, but station "B" actually has more listeners in the vitally important morning drive-time period of 6 a.m. to 10 a.m. Television station "X" has the largest share of the audience for its 6 p.m. newscast, but careful research behind the ratings book indicates that lower-rated tv station "Y" has a viewership that is more affluent, and therefore perhaps more desirable for prospective advertisers, than the competition's audience.

Researchers also investigate the likes and dislikes of audiences. Why do some people enjoy listening to one radio personality while other people do not? How does a sample audience react to a "pilot" episode of a potential new tv series? These kinds of measurements are very important to broadcasters and help determine the kinds of programs that will be offered on the air, and may be used to determine who is employed as the on-air talent for the programs.

Research and marketing experts look for competitive advantages in the demographics of audience ratings. They provide this kind of information to the Sales Department. In the often cut-throat business of broadcast sales, any competitive edge can be a cutting edge. Cutting off sales to the other stations and directing more advertising revenue to your own Sales Department.

All of these above job categories provide opportunities for entry-level employment at broadcast facilities. As you will read in the following pages determination to get into these kinds of jobs can be very rewarding.

Only a little less than three months after graduating from Kansas University, Kelly Howlett landed her first broadcasting job in the "real world." She is the Promotions Director of two Kansas City radio stations, KCMO-AM and KBKC-FM, both owned by Summit Communications, Inc., of North Carolina.

How does a recent college graduate cook up such an excellent "entry-level" job? With a big dose of personal confidence, a touch of aggressiveness, and...a dash; dashing to take advantage of possible opportunities.

"I graduated from K.U. in May, 1985 and was hired at the radio stations on August 12 of that year. I had been an intern at the stations before Summit Communications completed its purchase of them. That was over the Christmas recess of 1984-85.

"Because I was an intern I thought it would help me a lot to get a full-time job there. I wanted to be a sales representative. So, for two weeks I tracked down the FM Sales Manager. I called, and called, and called, and called. I thought, 'Well, they ought to want to talk with me. I've been there. I know what I'm doing and I know I can help them.'

"I kept trying to track down people, and finally I got in for an interview. But I found out that it really didn't help at all that I had been there because there was new management (due to the sale of the stations). I found out that new management doesn't care a whole heck of a lot about what the old management had done.

"But because I had been there earlier it gave me enough confidence that I thought it would help that I came in and pitched myself saying I really could do the job. I thought I would have a foot in the door that I actually didn't have.

"Yet the confidence I had from being here before helped me think they would want to talk with me. And, in fact they did want to talk with me after I got here.

"I had heard that lots of things were changing at the stations and that they would need people. I came in and applied for a position in sales as an account executive. As I was having my interview the new General Manager came in but I wasn't aware that he was the G.M.

"He was walking around and started joking around, and we discussed the radio station and a lot of the things that were going on. I was able to speak with him very well. We had a great conversation and a great interview.

"At the end of the interview I was asked, 'Why aren't you applying for the position as Promotions Director?' I told him I was not aware there was an opening for that position.

"He said, 'There is. Would you be interested?'

"And, I said, 'You bet I would be!'

"I was lucky enough to be offered the position—which I jumped at.

"My two week internship was in the Sales Department and I did everything. I went on sales calls, I wrote commercial copy, I read a lot of information. It was a very intensive two-week period.

"I really was allowed to do quite a bit of stuff around the station. I was allowed to write copy that went on the air. I sat in on every department to see how the radio station actually worked, not just how a college station works. There is a lot of difference as I'm finding every day. I got to do a lot in every department.

"Initially when I was hired it was with the understanding that pretty soon they would hire someone else to be Promotions Director of the AM station, but instead of doing that they have kept me working as Promotions Director of both stations and they hired a Marketing Director to also handle both stations.

"In my current job there is a lot of coordination between Promotions and the Programming and Sales Departments. We are kind of a liaison between the two.

''Soon after I started, my department put together two parties for listeners.

''The FM went on the air (with the new ownership) July 26, 1985 and I arrived at the station August 12. The first party I put together was a premier party and it was centered around the theme of the 'Dynasty' television show season premier. It was in a bar with big screen television sets to watch the shows. We had contests and even gave away a fur coat. It was a wonderful, excellent party. A big success.

''Then we had a Halloween party that was another huge success with costumes and a Halloween atmosphere and more prize give-aways.

''I am in charge of overseeing all the promotions that we do, making sure they get done and get done right. Making sure everything is scheduled and that everything happens when it's supposed to. This includes everything from on-the-air announcements to making sure the tables were correctly set up at the parties.

''If I need something I am able to draw on other people in the station to help me out. It's not like I'm an island unto myself here. But when it comes right down to getting things done, I have the responsibility to do them.

''I am learning so much. I have not yet instituted any promotions on my own except for the two parties. But, for example, our Program Director decides what he wants (for promotional events) and then I do it. I get a lot of guidance. They tell me how they want things done and if changes need to be made.

''For anyone thinking about getting a job in broadcasting I'd say that you have to believe in yourself and don't be afraid to show that. Not in an arrogant manner, but in a confident way. That's very important because nobody else is going to fight for you. Nobody else is going to believe in you because there are a million other students coming out of school that year who want that same job.

''You have to expect to deal with all types of people, get along with them, understand not everyone is like you are.

"Working at the college station pretty much prepared me for the business aspect of broadcasting. I knew how a radio station worked. I knew what the different departments were, what they did, and what they were there for. I was prepared to handle all those things.

"I think what people might not be prepared for is the person-to-person aspect of the business workplace. It is a lot different out in the 'real world' when you're dealing with people who've been working for 20 years compared to you who just came out of school after going to school for the last 20 years.

"The motivations are completely different. Completely. And I think that everybody has to expect to become harder and tougher, at least at work. You better or you're going to be eaten alive."

14

SELLING YOURSELF FOR A JOB IN BROADCAST SALES

*"Pleasant persistence
lowers resistance" vs.
"No guts, no glory!"*

BROADCASTING IS BUSINESS. Big business. Every year sponsors pump a combined total of more than $20 billion worth of advertising revenues into the nation's radio and television stations. That's a lot of fast food, laundry detergent, and used car commercials.

The advertising dollars pay the salaries of the radio and television station employees. The better the product the staff members send out over the airwaves, the higher the ratings. The higher the ratings, the happier the station's Sales Department because the rates they can charge for commercials directly depend on the size of the audience listening or viewing the programs.

Radio and tv sales representatives sell airtime usually in increments of 5, 10, 15, 30, and 60 seconds, the various lengths of live and pre-recorded commercials. Local merchants buy time to tout their goods and services. National and international companies do the same.

A good sales rep working at a highly-rated, major market tv station easily can annually earn more than $100,000 in commissions, getting a percentage of the advertising revenues he or she brings to the station. (A 30 second spot in the number one rated evening newscast in New York, Chicago, or Los Angeles will cost thousands of dollars.)

On the other hand, a poorly rated station in a small market may only be able to charge sponsors less than $100 per commercial during some parts of the day. A sales rep's commission of 5 or 8 percent certainly does not go as far on $100 sales as it does for prime time spots that sell for $3,000 or more each.

Recent Super Bowl telecast advertising rates were quoted at more than $1 million per commercial; however, when the rates go that high the sales representatives' commissions are sharply cut. Still, even a fraction of a percent of a million bucks isn't bad.

Some small market radio stations sell even their highest rated programs at only a few dollars per commercial. But then the cost of living in those communities is considerably less than in midtown Manhattan or Beverly Hills. Larger market radio stations will sell their spots at rates up to hundreds of dollars per minute, and for special broadcasts such as local NFL football games, the station may demand well over $1,000 for 60 seconds worth of airtime.

Sales reps may move around from station to station and town to town as frequently as some on-the-air staff members. If the sales rep does well for a station in Boston, the owner of the station may want to send the rep to the company's station in San Diego to help boost sales revenues there.

Traditionally, a good track record in broadcast sales can lead to management positions. A good sales rep can seek a promotion to the post of General Sales Manager. Doing well in that job, the next step is General Manager of the station itself, then perhaps a post higher in the company overseeing sales in an entire region of the country or being in charge of several stations owned by one company.

Continual promotions are good for the bank account, but they may involve frequently changing banks. One top industry executive, for example, graduated from Central Michigan University and went to work in Los Angeles in 1962. Between 1962 and 1974 he held various sales posts in the same company and moved from L.A. to Chicago, St. Louis, and New York. For seven years he ably served as Vice President and General Manager of WEEI-AM in Boston. Since 1981 he again has been based in New York.

It is an excellent track record, but it did require plenty of moving around the country.

Here is another example of how selling people on your abilities can lead to sales success in broadcasting.

In a little more than a decade, Ithaca College broadcasting graduate Junior Winokur, a native of Philadelphia, skyrocketed from a job shuffling announcer's copy and program logs to General Sales Manager of two prominent, major market radio stations. To do it, she moved around the country going from Chicago, to New York, back to Chicago, and now her current job is based in San Francisco where she is General Sales Manager of KCBS Radio.

"There is no such thing as luck. It's all hard work," she emphasizes.

To get her first broadcasting job after college Winokur had to use some "hard sell."

"I graduated from Ithaca College in June, 1972 and moved to Chicago in January, 1973. I didn't have the guts to move to New York City. I was really terrified of it. And, I didn't think I wanted California. I knew some people who said Chicago was really good for broadcasting, so I thought, 'It's in the middle of the country, why not?'

"I started as a Traffic Manager at WLAK-FM in Chicago. That was my first broadcasting job, but first I had started graduate school and worked as the manager of a furniture sales showroom at the Merchandise Mart (a huge Chicago building filled with furniture wholesale and retail showrooms, and for many years the Chicago headquarters of NBC). I ran the showroom for six months because I couldn't find any broadcasting jobs.

"I got a Masters Degree in Industrial Relations at Loyola University because I thought about going into law school, but I ran out of money and energy.

"I found a job at WLAK in 'Ad Week' magazine. I was not, of course, the only one to apply for that job, and the ad said: 'Wanted—Traffic Manager. One year of experience mandatory.'

"When I went to see the station's General Manager and give my whole little pitch, I said, 'Look, I don't have a year's experience, however, I've got four years of college working in broadcasting, and I did traffic for two stations. So four years of college equals one year in the real world!'

"He thought it was a pretty good angle. I also told him that I was smart enough so that whatever most people would take six weeks to learn, I could learn in three, that I was a very quick study. And, I said that if I didn't learn in three weeks what he thought I should learn then I wouldn't have to work there if he didn't want me to.

"No guts, no glory!

"When I worked traffic at Ithaca the stations were both commercial. It was WICB-AM and FM. The AM was on carrier-current (essentially closed circuit) just for the college, but the FM was for the whole city.

"When I finally got the WLAK job, I realized that what I had learned doing traffic at Ithaca was absolutely adequate for preparing me for the real world.

"I worked at WLAK for two and a half years. Back then, in 1973—the 'old days'—there were no computers in use at the stations. So, everything was all done manually. All the notations on the program log were entered by hand and the copy was all put in order manually.

"I had a four foot by five foot piece of cardboard on the wall that I worked horizontally and vertically with all the commercials for seven days marked on it. I had different smaller boards with different colors to mark things like sponsorships; red for business program sponsorships, green for commuter traffic reports, and so on. So, we didn't miss anything. We had checks and balances.

"I added some improvements to the system so that we made sure nothing would fall through the cracks.

"After that job, I went to NBC and sold advertising time for what was then WNIS-FM (now WKQX-FM), the infamous News and Information Service (an all-news experiment by NBC Radio that was optimistically launched and then quickly folded in the mid-1970s).

"It took me over a year to get into that sales job. I pitched every single General Manager and General Sales Manager in Chicago. I went to talk with all of them explaining 'Here's why I'm the greatest, why I'd be terrific.'

"And they all told me, 'You're cute, too, but come back when you have some experience.' This was back in 1974 and 1975 and there were very, very few women in broadcasting sales. Maybe two or three in Chicago.

"So, it took me a really long time to find a believer. The person who ultimately hired me is a legend in the business, Charlie Warner. I guess I was aggressive enough and positive enough that they figured, 'I guess she's worth a shot.'

"But before him everyone else said, 'Yeah, you'd be terrific, but come back when you get some experience.'

"It took me over a year to find somebody who would say, 'We'll give you the experience.' I just kept going. Kept going until I found someone.

"I was with WNIS exactly a year to the day I got hired. I then joined CBS Radio Spot Sales in Chicago. I did that for ten months and then got transferred to CBS Radio Spot Sales in New York and was there for not quite two years.

"Then I became Local Sales Manager at WCBS-AM in New

York and did that for not quite two years. Then I went back to CBS Radio Spot Sales as the New York Sales Manager and did that for two and a half years.

"From there I went to WBBM-AM in Chicago as General Sales Manager. I was there for about two years, and now I'm General Sales Manager at KCBS-AM in San Francisco.

"Sometimes people tell me that I'm lucky (to go from her first commercial broadcasting job to Sales Manager of some of the biggest radio stations in the country in less than a decade). But I say there is no such thing as luck. It's all hard work.

"If I had to do it over again, I don't know if I would make as many moves. In a way it's good that I did because I kept moving up, new challenges, and I kept growing (personally and professionally). But on the other hand, I think there is something to be said about staying with a job for four or five years.

"For any woman thinking about getting into broadcasting, I would say absolutely, positively do not start out as a secretary. Unfortunately, the way the 'male chauvinist mind' works, once a secretary, always a secretary. You're never seen on an equal level anyway, but if you're a secretary you're seen on an even more unequal level. That's really feminist to say, but it is true.

"Get into some sales-related area. A sales support area, such as Traffic or Continuity. Just don't be a secretary, even if the job description calls it 'Sales Assistant.' Don't.

"For men or women who want to get into broadcasting sales, my watchword has been: 'Pleasant persistence lowers resistance.' It's really true, whether you're out there trying to get your first job, or you're out there trying to get your first sales order or your hundredth order.

"It's a very competitive business and we're all basically fighting for either the same (employment) positions or the same pieces of pie (the available advertising revenue). The squeaky wheel gets the grease, but you can be aggressive without being obnoxious. If you just pleasantly persist you will eventually lower their resistance so that you either a) get hired, or b) get the (sales) order.

"I don't know that it really matters if someone starts by looking for a job in a small market or a large one. If somebody is good then they will, by their nature, move on their own. They will get recognized.

"If you're in Keokuk, Iowa then maybe don't stay there too long. But whatever and wherever the first job is, I always say stay in that first job no matter how bad it is, no matter how small the station is. Stay in it at least a year.

"There are a lot of reasons. The first three or four months of a new job don't count because you don't even know where the Ladies' Room or Men's Room is.

"Then you're learning how to sell, and then in your last three months of that year you'll probably be doing it pretty well.

"In this business, especially in sales, people tend to make a lot of moves. It is very checkerboard. It's pretty much expected that that's what people do and it's not frowned on or looked at really terribly. But if you make too many moves especially in the beginning, at least to me, it shows a lack of stability.

"I would look at someone who moved around a lot early in their career and say, 'If you made this many moves and you had made a commitment to your first job and yet didn't even stay a year, then how do I know you're not going to do the same thing to me if I hire you?

"You should always stay in your first job at least a year to garner the experience. Then you can always move to another local station, or move to another market.

"I have hired people who had no broadcast sales experience, but did have sales experience elsewhere. That brings me to another expression I often use: 'What we do is not brain surgery.'

"Selling skills are the most important thing. The product is the easiest thing to learn. You really can't teach someone how to sell. They have to have the basics, and if they really have those basics, and the instincts and the guts and all that good stuff, then it is easy to teach them the product (the attributes of the radio or television station).

15

HIGH FINANCE AND
HIGH HOPES

*"Business has become very
competitive and
broadcasting is business."*

As You Have read in earlier chapters, not everyone now in broadcasting started out with the goal of entering the industry. For one reason or another they were hired by radio or television stations, cable systems, or broadcasting related companies.

As I was writing this chapter I was reminded of a television station publicity department worker who originally wanted to be an actor. He could not find enough acting jobs to pay the rent and grocery bills, but he was able to find a public relations job. Rather than take more chances being turned down for acting roles, he stayed with broadcasting P.R. work.

This brief chapter will show how people can sometimes achieve top jobs at top broadcasting facilities even though a few years earlier they might have laughed at the very idea of one day holding that kind of industry position.

Beneath Wayne Jefferson's impeccable pin-stripe suit and crisp white shirt beats the heart of rock 'n' roll and a dry sense of humor that erupts frequently with a big grin.

Jefferson began life-after-college as an up-and-coming pencil pusher, an accountant with a prestigious New York company. But this otherwise intelligent man kept looking at possible job openings behind the scenes in the entertainment field.

When Jefferson started his accounting career he secretly desired to be involved in the recording industry, but he never dreamed that in a few years he would be in command of a major market radio station that was playing those "hot hits." Today, Wayne Jefferson is Vice President and General Manager of WBBM-FM in Chicago. More than a million listeners a week tune in to hear the contemporary sounds of "B-96," making it one of the most popular stations in the country's third largest market.

"In school at New York University I was a business major; business, finance and accounting with a second major in marketing. After graduating I went into public accounting at Price Waterhouse Company and while there I expressed an interest in the entertainment field—the record industry.

"I had thought about [accounting work in] radio and tv, but I really liked the record industry more. While at Price Waterhouse I wound up with a lot of broadcasting clients, doing audits and financial reviews, special projects and Securities and Exchange Commission filing work for companies such as Westinghouse.

"I also had another very large client, Interpublic Group of Companies, Inc., a holding company for advertising companies such as McCann-Erickson. That led back into broadcasting, too.

"In my third year there I more or less got tired of working seven days a week, 60 or 70 hours a week, and decided to leave. But I was talked into staying for one more year and was given all new clients—one of them in the Bahamas. . . .

"I was one of the hot shots. I had the best client list in the New York office. I was doing fine. I just didn't like the work. It was a little bit of fun for one year, but at the end of that year I made up my mind that I was definitely going to leave public accounting and I started looking around for a new job, hopefully at a broadcasting firm.

"CBS was my first choice. CBS has always been viewed as Number One, the blue chip broadcaster and record company. I lucked out. I knew a couple of people who had accounting or financial jobs there, and I wound up in the CBS Internal Audit Department. That was a corporate department. At first I had nothing to do with records or broadcasting. My preference back then was still the record industry over broadcasting.

"But while working at this corporate function I sort of drifted into the position of being the department's broadcasting specialist. I wrote financial programs and approaches to reviewing the businesses and did a lot of work involving CBS radio and television stations, entertainment operations and CBS Sports.

"I stayed in that function for about seven years. Most of that time I was trying to find what I considered a 'good' job in records. But at that time —the early 1970's—the record industry really went on a blank and there didn't appear to be very much work, security, longevity or opportunity or anything else in records. Being a flexible type of guy I started looking closer at broadcasting.

"I had been lucky enough to meet a lot of people in broadcasting over the years and I started to express an interest to these people. As luck would have it, I was in charge of a staff that was doing a financial audit of WBBM-AM in Chicago. When the audit was over, there were some staff changes at the station, I was offered a job.

"I went there [in 1982] as Director of Administration and worked very closely with the General Managers of both WBBM-AM and FM, and when the General Manager of the FM eventually transferred back to the East Coast to Boston I was fortunate enough to be offered this position [as V.P./G.M. of WBBM-FM].

"I've been lucky because the three years I was in the radio station's finance department [as Director of Administration], I worked really closely on things such as contractual negotiations, dealings with advertising agencies, quite a few business-oriented tasks and work with the sales staffs, not just debits and credits, the number crunching. So, therefore, I became very familiar with the workings of both the AM and the FM radio stations, more than many finance people might become.

"The way it worked out, I was almost in a training position for three years.

"Although I don't admit it a lot, I 'demoted' myself to move from New York to Chicago to take the job [as Director of Administration]. I assumed that if I got into an operational position at a radio station that I could get very good training, get experience, and eventually be in line for an upper managerial position at a station somewhere. It just so happened it was also in Chicago. And, in a shorter period of time than I thought would have been possible. Luck!

"Today in broadcasting, and I guess in any other kind of industry, it is a day of specialization, and also a day of the 'seasoned' and experienced, creative person or a straight business and managerial type person. Business has become very competitive and broadcasting is business. So you have to plan; you have to make choices.

"You have to make a decision, at least a general type of decision, to be a creative or an announcer type of person, or become the head of finance or a sales person, and then find out what the normal path is, the normal career track.

"Generally, that means starting off a smaller stations where you get to see more of the operations and you'll slowly get experience and sort of work your way up through several job changes. From what I've seen, that works better than anything else.

"Get good experience from some place, and then you can convince the world that you have some abilities. But seasoning and exposure are what you need, and planning from a personal point of view about what you want.''

16

MAKING A BIG PRODUCTION WITH YOUR CAREER — PART ONE

"If you have a neighbor or a relative who has a second cousin who lives in California, then get that person's name and call."

HUNDREDS OF COMPANIES across the country are involved in broadcasting but do not actually broadcast anything themselves. These include huge television and film studios like Paramount, very successful radio program and music concert packagers like Westwood One (which now owns the Mutual radio network), and "boutique" houses that specialize in making commercials, providing on-location equipment and personnel, and various production and distribution services. The networks, individual radio and tv stations, and even individual sponsors or their advertising agencies purchase the goods and services of these other companies.

Anyone interested in a career in broadcasting should not be limited to just searching for work at radio or tv station. There are many possibilities for entry-level jobs at broadcast related companies. And, when the radio and tv stations slash their budgets and their staff sizes because of mergers (ABC now is merged with Capital Cities Communications and NBC merged with General Electric) or other financial considerations, the stations often depend on these outside vendors to provide the same kinds of services and programming they used to produce with their own facilities and employees.

There are jobs for production assistants (a position that can range from glorified gopher to more important responsibilities), researchers who check the accuracy of tv game show quiz questions, graphics artists, animators, librarians, videotext operators (who type stories, scores, and other information that is shown on television screens on cable tv systems, for example), and scriptwriters.

On the technical end, you'll find positions as floor managers, electricians, carpenters, stagehands who move props, video and audio tape editors, film projectionists, and jobs involving sound, lighting, and camera related operations.

Many of these production companies advertise job openings in trade publications such as "Millimeter," a monthly magazine that covers the motion picture and television production industries. A later chapter lists some of these magazines and other sources of information about potential job openings.

However, many jobs in the industry are obtained by having the right connections, knowing someone who knows someone else who is looking to fill a vacancy on a staff somewhere. Having "contacts" in the industry never hurts and usually is very important for finding future jobs as well as your first one.

Making those contacts literally can begin in your backyard. Perhaps a neighbor knows someone somewhere who is involved in the industry. A friend, a teacher, a member of the clergy, anyone might have some remote contacts that can lead to a job interview. It depends on your own determination and ingenuity.

Determination is a word—and concept—that must never be forgotten by anyone who really wants a job in broadcasting or wants to advance to another job in the industry. Sometimes determination also takes guts.

———————————

Ramona Layman has guts. At the age of 28 "Mona" quit a good-paying position as a newswriter at one of the biggest radio stations in Chicago, packed her belongings, and moved to the Los Angeles area without any other jobs lined up. She was determined to find some position in the television entertainment industry.

Not only did she find an interesting job—with a fringe benefit of meeting comedian Flip Wilson and even watching television at the home of singer/actress Gladys Knight—Layman has been successfully using her first Hollywood work to line up future jobs in the industry.

"My present title is Production Assistant for the CBS-TV program 'Charlie & Company' produced by Twentieth Century Fox Productions. I work everyday on the studio lot of KABC-TV.

"I remember the first time I saw Flip Wilson. I had been asked to go upstairs and tell him to come downstairs for a rehearsal. I went to his dressing room and knocked on the door.

"It was kind of a shock. I had met famous people before while working in news, but never actually got to know someone for more than a few minutes. My first meeting with Flip Wilson was kind of a shock, kind of 'Wow! He's a star and I've seen him for 15 years and I never thought I'd be working with him.'

"But as the weeks progressed it was like professionally working with anybody. I am not awe-struck anymore.

"The first time I met Gladys Knight we were in the elevator together and I had no idea what to expect. She is probably the nicest person at the show. I introduced myself because I was going to be around the set and I wanted her to know who I was. Part of my job is to have the cast and crew call on me if they need anything.

''One day I delivered a script to her house and wound up watching 'Magnum P.I.' with her when she invited me in!

''This is my very first television production job in California. The way I got it is I went to dinner with a friend and she introduced me at the dinner to the Associate Producer of the program. The Associate Producer was looking for someone to fill in for two weeks on the show in place of the Production Co-Ordinator. It was just a fill-in job to answer the phones or do whatever else they wanted to have done.

''I said, 'Sure, I'll do it!' because I was working temporary jobs and looking for any kind of 'in' for a broadcasting job. I said, 'Hey, why not?' and I did it.

''After I got the job, the Associate Producer said: 'We can use another Production Assistant, why don't you stay on board.' And I did.

''When I packed up and moved to Los Angeles the only people I knew personally out here were a brother of a friend and a sister of a friend, and they really didn't have any film or television connections.''

Layman explains that a veteran staff member of the radio station back in Chicago passed along the names of a few potential California contacts. The staff member, John Madigan, is the father of award-winning actress Amy Madigan and father-in-law of award-winning actor Ed Harris.

''Unfortunately, those names of contacts did not pan out very well. The names were people that Ed Harris had worked with on a new film, ''Sweet Dreams,'' and he passed the names along to Amy and she gave them to John and he gave them to me.

''When I got to California I called all these people. They were all friendly, but there was nothing available. They said nothing was happening just then, they would keep me in mind and I should send a resume. There was no problem that I was calling them on a recommendation from Ed Harris.

''So I signed up with some temporary help agencies and did clerical work. Typing, filing, whatever, just something to make some money to keep me going until I got a job.

''And, I was lucky! Everybody tells me I was lucky because

I got a job after I had only been out here about six or seven weeks. And, it was because I went to dinner with one of the two people I knew.

"The sister of a friend asked me to come to dinner with her because her sister—my friend from back home—was going to be in town. So we all went to have dinner, and coincidently the Associate Producer from 'Charlie & Company' was there, too.

"Now, the woman who asked me to come to dinner was not introducing me as someone who wanted to get a job. The Associate Producer was just a friend of hers and it was just supposed to be all of us getting together for dinner.

"During the course of dinner, though, the subject came up. I said I was looking for work and was willing to do anything to get connections because you need connections before you really can get a good job.

"Generally, Production Assistants do a lot of running. They deliver scripts, they deliver tapes, they pick up things. But, then the Associate Producer gave me a little more responsibility. I take care of some books, the purchase orders, and I match them up with invoices and keep a record of all those. I take care of changes in the scripts when the Script Supervisor says changes need to be done. I do some typing and get them to the actors.

"I do carry around an awful lot of paper. 'Here are some changes for THIS page,' I say to the cast and crew quite often.

"It is generally a little bit more than a Production Assistant usually does, but the Associate Producer likes me, so she has given me more responsibilities connected to the business end of the show.

"I've talked to quite a few people about this and they say there is no way I could have gone into a Production Co-Ordinator job without the experience I've been getting. The more you're around [the production studio set], the more you learn and you make a lot of connections on the job. I've met quite a few people through the actors and production people I've met on the set. Directors, Stage Managers, the Production Co-Ordinator. They've all introduced me to other people and that can easily lead to other jobs in the future.

"There were two job interviews I did earlier that did not work out, but because of the interviews I now know several people at other TV shows, "Comedy Break" (a syndicated, half-hour comedy series), and "Night Court." The Production Co-Ordinator (from "Charlie & Co.") introduced me to people at these other shows. She knew these people from her previous jobs.

"So, I've only been in one job, but I know people in a lot of different shows because of contacts.

"For anyone who wants a job in network television production I would say definitely move out to Los Angeles, but it is a matter of luck to really meet somebody who can help you find a job. If you have a neighbor or a relative who has a second cousin who lives in California, then get that person's name and call. They may not be working directly in the entertainment field, but they may have their own contacts.

"Before I came out here a friend gave me the name of her mother's neighbor whose son-in-law worked on the Universal Studios lot. He was in charge of tours. He had nothing really to do with actual television programs or movies, but he was kind enough to gave me a list of names of possible contacts in California.

"Those people now have my name, and it may not work out right now for a job, but you need a lot of connections for the future.

"So, if you know a lawyer whose second cousin works out here [in Los Angeles], then get the name.

"And, you have to be willing to take a low-paying job and work a lot of long hours, that's just the nature of the business. I get to work about 8:30 in the morning and depending on the day of the week I leave the set at either 7 or 7:30 and some days at 9:00. On the days we videotape the program, I'm there until 10:00 at night.

"The hours are long, but the work really isn't that hard. I don't lift heavy boxes all day long. We stand around a lot and 'schmooz,' talk.

"If you really want to get involved in television entertainment production, don't wait. I waited until I was 28 to make the change. Newswriting was not my goal, but it was a starting point for me, something that happened after college. I always wanted to come out to California, but it was frightening to actually move away from your family, but you have to be here to get the jobs.

"You hear things from other people here that you never would hear about unless you're here. Possible other jobs at other studios. You would not hear about these jobs or meet these people sitting back home. The more people you know, the better.

"I'm happy I did it!"

As mentioned earlier, in addition to Twentieth Century Fox where Mona Laymon works on "Charlie & Company," there literally are hundreds of companies in the United States that provide production services and programs to individual radio and television stations, networks, and cable systems. Some of them have very familiar names, such as Columbia Pictures Television Distribution, Viacom International Inc., and Paramount Television Distribution.

The names of most of the others may not be familiar, but all of them should be viewed as potential places of broadcasting or broadcast-related employment.

Award-winning producer John Cosgrove works for one of those many companies. A member of the Directors Guild of America (DGA), he is Vice President of DBA Communications, Inc., Los Angeles, an independent film production company that is part of Dave Bell Associates, Inc.

A complete listing of Cosgrove's industry achievements would run several pages, but here is a brief synopsis: He has won a dozen Emmys from the Los Angeles chapter of the National Academy of Television Arts and Sciences and more than two dozen national and international film festival awards. These include Gold Awards from the International TV Festival of New York and the Milan, Italy, Film Festival for "Angel Death," a landmark documentary dealing with the drug PCP, starring Paul Newman and Joanne Woodward.

His HBO film, "Five American Guns," was the first made-for-cable movie to be selected for special screening by the Academy and won top awards in competition in New York, San Francisco, and Montreal.

In addition, Cosgrove has worked as an executive producer, director and/or writer on television programs broadcast on ABC ("The National Save-A-Life Test" with Michael Learned and Bernie Kopell) and NBC (a series of highly-acclaimed specials on missing persons).

"I was an English major in college and, like many people, wondered what I was going to do with that kind of a degree. I was interested in writing, so I went to graduate school to study television and film. It clicked. That was in 1967.

"I went into the Peace Corps and the best part about the Peace Corps was that I was able to get a lot of hands-on experience in writing and producing a program in Kingston, Jamaica that taught adult illiterates how to read and write. I also had the opportunity to make a recruiting and training film for the Peace Corps. Those were my first 'credits.'

"When I came back to the United States I had some reels under my arm that I could show people. One of the first things you need to do is have something you can show prospective employers. Find any way you can to be involved in a production at any level so that when you walk into someone's office looking for a job you've got something you can leave behind that is an example of your work."

Cosgrove says he obtained his first job after leaving the Peace Corps by banging on doors and using contacts he had made earlier.

"It was a matter of friends I had made in graduate school. They told me about job leads. I started as an Assistant Editor, I also worked as an assistant on shooting with the camera and worked my way up that way. I learned by working in the boiler room.

"My first job was synching up film (synchronizing the sound portion of the film with the video portion during the editing process). My second job was helping to write a local television station's responses to challenges to their FCC license. This is the kind of work that is very unglamorous, but you do learn the business from inside.

"I worked freelance for KNBC-TV and KNXT-TV (now KCBS-TV) in Los Angeles doing odd jobs. I worked with people who then ultimately became my partners at Dave Bell Associates.

"But it all started with contacts I made in graduate school. The friendships that you make along the way through networking ultimately lead to jobs.

"There are not many entry-level positions in our company. Generally, we are looking for skilled people to fill jobs. What we've done, however, is set up internships, something many companies are doing. College students come in to work part-time without pay for two, three or four days a week.

"They get college credits for their work and get a chance to see how the business works, and we get a chance to see them. We've had people who've started out as Interns and in two or three years have worked their way up to become Field Producers.

"Aside from internship programs at individual broadcasting stations and companies, the communications schools have these kinds of programs and so do the Academy of National Television Arts and Sciences and the Directors Guild."

Cosgrove points out that with so many different production companies in operation there are many different routes job-seekers can take.

"It is an entirely different population, group of people, in theatrical movies than those who work in made-for-tv movies. Then there's an entirely different population of people who hire for syndicated television programs (those sold directly to individual tv stations), in local television, network and cable television.

"I think there is a lot of opportunity with independent companies. If someone comes to Los Angeles looking for a job they should pick up a copy of one of the directories listing all the production companies and networks, get on the phone, and line up job interviews.

"It does help to have contacts. You have to develop a network.

That's the key. Somebody you talk to may not have an opening but might give you three other names you can contact. This way your list of contacts grows and grows.

"The people I know who work freelance spend probably a third of their time working on setting up their next job.

"I believe that the best job anyone can get to start out in television is to be a Page at one of the networks. If you have a Masters Degree you might think that's menial work, but I know so many people who started out as Pages and now are Vice Presidents of different companies. It is phenomenal.

"Meet as many people as you can find to get that entry-level job."

17

MAKING A BIG PRODUCTION WITH YOUR CAREER— PART TWO

"I don't think anyone can succeed in this business unless they've been fired two or three times."

THE MOST COMMON on-air broadcasting jobs, not including soap opera and entertainment tv series acting, are the local radio and tv jobs for disc jockeys, talk show hosts, and the usual news, weather and sports positions. With more than 11,400 commercial and non-commercial broadcasting outlets in the United States that is where the majority of on-air positions are found.

People with specialized expertise outside of broadcasting may be able to find part-time or full-time employment based on their outside knowledge.

A personable meteorologist should not hestitate to knock on the doors at radio and tv stations seeking an on-air job as the station's exclusive weather forecaster. I know of two meteorologists who started doing part-time work giving the forecasts several times a day on radio stations and within a few years they had built an entire network of stations in the Midwest and East that carried their forecasts tailored specifically to the stations' listening areas.

Agriculture is a frequent topic on small and medium sized market radio and tv stations. More than 200 radio stations in the U.S. devote substantial portions of their programming to agriculture and farming. Often the stations have a "Farm Reporter" or at least a "Farm Report" several times during the day when agriculture news is presented on the air. Expertise in this area can be a strong selling point when applying for a job with a station that serves the agricultural community.

About 500 radio stations have all-news or news and talk show formats. More than 700 stations regularly broadcast religion-oriented programs. Many radio and television stations will use specialists either full-time or part-time in the areas of medicine, religion, and entertainment, such as movie and theatrical play reviews.

Part-time jobs reporting the morning and afternoon rush-hour traffic conditions may be available. In several larger cities, private companies have formed local networks to provide highway traffic information to radio and tv stations in their communities. These companies often hire eager people who are seeking entry-level positions. Some of these employees have then graduated to full-time jobs at stations in those towns.

One college graduate student pursuing a doctorate in pscyhology frequently worked for small market radio stations conducting audience opinion research. The surveys were quantitative measurements as well as qualitative surveys to determine listeners' attitudes and buying habits. The results of the research were valuable tools for the radio station's limited sales staff.

The Health & Science Reporter of a major Midwest tv station has a Ph.D. in biology. At a competing station in that same city, the Health & Science specialist has "D.D.S." after his name, but has not practiced dentistry for several years because of his many tv reporting duties.

One of the prominent correspondents on the network tv "magazine format'' program ''West 57th St.,'' Bob Sirott, earlier worked as the Lifestyle Reporter for a major market tv station. Before that he was a successful disc jockey.

A political science professor from a university serves as a tv station's on-the-air analyst for foreign affairs stories including Middle East terrorism.

Spanish language programming on tv stations in the country's larger cities is commonplace now. There also are tv programs, including newscasts, being broadcast in other languages besides English and Spanish. French, German, Italian, Polish, and Portuguese can be heard regularly on radio stations around the country.

There is much more to radio and tv programming than a dozen different kinds of music, news and talk formats, game shows, soap operas, and the evening eyewitness newscast. Don't limit your expectations to just one small part of the business. Don't be oblivious to the many potential jobs throughout the entire industry. You never know when your career can take an unexpected turn, for better or worse, and if you can't be at the right place at the right time, you at least want to know where those right places might be located in the future.

Being at the right place at the right time has been very rewarding for Robb Weller, the co-host of the highly-rated, syndicated ''Entertainment Tonight'' (ET) and ''Entertainment This Week'' (ETW) television programs. More than 140 stations broadcast the daily program.

''ET'' and ''ETW'' are produced in the same way the nightly newscasts are put together. The content of the show can drastically change right up until the weekday deadline at 12:45 p.m. Los Angeles time when it is prepared to be fed across the country by satellite.

Like any major news organization, the show is staffed around the clock. The main production team arrives for work at about 4:15 in the morning. Robb Weller says he ''strolls in'' at about

7:00 and immediately goes into story meetings, starts recording voice-over narrations in recording booths, and is continually updating stories and attending meetings for the next four hours.

The programs are videotaped at Paramount Studios, the same place where "Cheers" and "Solid Gold" are produced along with other successful tv programs.

"Going to lunch at the Paramount commissary is indeed a trip. They made the original 'King Kong' on our set," acknowledges Weller with his typical wide-eyed humor.

After taping the day's "ET" program, Weller takes a lunch break of several hours, then returns for more meetings and time on the telephone checking on stories. He often goes out with a camera crew in the evening at a premier or film screening to get a story for the next day's show.

"Although it's Hollywood, let's be honest. I am not in my jacuzzi by 1:30 p.m.," says Weller with a laugh.

But Weller readily admits his fast-paced and glamourous career has not been filled only with successes.

"I did a show in New York called 'Two On The Town,' an evening news magazine which just did not make it. I don't know what New Yorkers wanted, but believe me, what I gave them they did not want," he recalls.

Weller's own talents, coupled with industry contacts, luck, and even a double case of mistaken identity, have propelled his career from doing half-time football broadcasts in hometown Seattle to hosting daily television programs in Columbus, Ohio, Chicago, New York, and now Hollywood. And, it has all happened in just a little over a decade.

"I had a really very, very bizarre beginning. I grew up in Seattle and in college I had been a yell leader and very active in a lot of alumni things. I was the Master of Ceremonies for a lot of the alumni rallies and dinners and the weekly quarterback and coaches luncheon meetings. So, I had become sort of a bit of a celebrity through that and some of the broadcasters knew me.

"One of the broadcasters decided to add someone on the sidelines for coverage of the football games, and since I knew so many of the players they gave me a buzz.

"I started doing some radio there for a few weeks doing University of Washington 'Huskies' football broadcasts from the sidelines. I'd listen to what the quarterback and the coach were talking about and would be able to get in one or two comments per quarter on the radio.

"I earned $52 a week for the game, and they also let me do a pre-game show from up in the stands for another $52. I couldn't believe it, I was so thrilled!

"I did that for a couple of weeks, and then things started to snowball. I was asked to fill in for the morning sports fellow on KING-TV while he was on vacation for a week. It was the first tv work I had ever done. The same afternoon that the television station called, an advertising agency called me and I became a spokesman for a local department store.

"It was Bing, Bang, Boom, and I thought, 'Hey, this is the easiest business in the world!' But eventually, you learn it's not so easy.

"During the next year I was hired to do a part-time public affairs show on KING-TV, and after about a year I got a phone call from a fella in Columbus, Ohio. He said, 'Robb, I want you to come out here and audition for Warner CUBE,' an experimental cable television system.

"They had been advertising in Broadcasting magazine for a job opening in Columbus, and they got an audition tape that had the name Milt Friedman on it. They looked at the tape and really liked what they saw, thinking it was Friedman. They called him and asked him to come to Ohio and audition.

"But Friedman explained he was the Producer, the person they want to meet is the host of the program on the audition tape, Cliff Winn. They were very embarrassed and called Cliff and asked him to come out and audition.

"Cliff was very excited. He made plans to use some vacation time to go out to Columbus. But about a week before he was scheduled to go out there, someone back in Ohio completely rewound his audition tape to the beginning.

"When they started playing the tape the announcer came on and said, 'Welcome to Seattle Today with Cliff and Shirley,' and as the audience is applauding Shirley comes on and says, 'Cliff is on vacation. Filling in is Robb Weller.'

"So, unbeknownst to me, this tape had been sent to Ohio eight or nine months earlier, and the people in Columbus thought I was actually two other people—first, Milt, then Cliff. Out of nowhere they called and asked me to come out and audition.

"I auditioned and got the job. But at any point, they could have been so embarrassed they could have said, 'Forget it, we'll just take the other guy, or someone else.'

"I worked about eight months in Columbus doing a talk show there on the interactive cable tv system. Then all of a sudden they went through some financial problems and people were either being fired or bailing out on their own left and right. Suddenly our General Manager was gone, too.

"About two weeks later, I get a phone call from him and he's the Program Manager at WLS-TV in Chicago. He said the host of 'AM Chicago' who had only been there briefly had been removed from the show, and they wanted me to come in and audition. I flew up there, auditioned, and a week later was called and told I had the job.

"So, all of a sudden I went from the 34th largest market to the number two market at that time as the morning tv talk show host.

"So, I really got into the whole business on a quirk. But you start meeting people [who can help you later in your career].

"One of the great quotes we use around the office all the time is: 'There are only 37 people in the entire business and we just all keep working for each other.'

"Once you break into that circle you find there are different strata. You get into the local scene and everyone knows all the local people. You get into the news scene and everyone knows all the news people. If you are lucky enough to get a national break here or there you find there is sort of a little network of people there, too.

"I was just incredibly lucky.

"I was host of 'AM Chicago' for five years and then went off to New York. That was the wrong place at the wrong time. In the face of adversity is when you really learn the true essence of show business. I don't think anyone can succeed in this business unless they've been fired two or three times. It sort of teaches you that there is life after the job you had worked so hard to get.

"I didn't learn that until I lost my job in New York. My first reaction was, 'Oh, no, it's all over.' Then you begin to realize that you have experience, you can build on it, and you go for the next job.

"The fella who hired me for 'ET' was an upperclassman I knew at the University of Washington. He used to look over my shoulder during some of the examinations in communications classes we were in together. He hired me as a reporter for 'ET.' That must come under the realm of charity.

"The New York program was a major extravaganza. 'AM Chicago' was very nice with a staff of six people and a wonderful show. The New York show had a staff of 34 people and backed by CBS in New York with a huge advertising budget. I remember we did two commercials for the show before we went on the air, and the production costs for the two was $100,000 and that just blew me away. What a budget!

"We thought the show had everything going for it. It just goes to show you can't count on anything in the business. You just sort of have to let it carry you like a big wave, you have to ride it. Sometimes it carries you into the shallows, sometimes it gives you a great curl, and in New York my wave took me right into the rocks. But I kept my head above water.

"But that won't be the last time that happens to me. This is a crazy business, and as long as you want to pursue the risks of trying to achieve something, the more your chances are of landing on your keester.

"After 'Two On The Town' I started with 'ET' as a reporter in New York. Shortly thereafter, I was hauled out to the West Coast to fill in for the then current co-host. While he was on vacation his contract expired and he walked out. I was filling in for him. Two weeks later they came to me and said, 'Congratulations, you're the new guy.'

"And, I said, 'Who, me?!' And, hence, history was made, and I got steady work.

"I lucked out in Columbus and Chicago. There are a lot of talented people out there who haven't had the breaks and they should.

"The key is, when you finally get a break and you sit down to do that audition—and we all have to audition—you just have to have composure and confidence.

"I learned in Columbus, Ohio where we could almost count all of our viewers on two hands, that you have to get all of the bad shows out of your system. I don't think anything beats a small market for experience. There are usually not many union restrictions. It allows you, if you want, to work camera one day; then, if you want to write, you can write a script, or you can try to direct. Your options are much more wide open at lower levels in smaller markets because they are glad to have you and you're glad to have the experience.

"The higher you get in the markets, the less you can do. I learned that in Chicago when I was not even allowed to put on my microphone or move an ashtray on the set; those are two separate unions, engineers and stagehands.

"I am a big proponent of working first in smaller markets. It worked for me going from small markets on up. It is also where you can have your most fun."

18

WHERE TO START LOOKING

*"Send tape and resume
to...."*

EVERY WEEK, THERE are Help Wanted advertisements
in broadcast industry publications, ads that usually seek experienced
applicants, but often there are ads that may read: "Experience
preferred but qualified entry-level applicants will be considered."

Some broadcasting managers realize lack of experience should
not completely prohibit someone from being reviewed for a job
opening. (Recall the story of Columbus, Ohio tv reporter Howard
Epstein in chapter nine. Without any previous television experience
he was able to land a reporter's job based on his current abilities
and talents.)

Many of the jobs immediately available to applicants with little
or no experience will be found in smaller markets. Frequently the
ads will say something like "excellent climate," "good hunting

and fishing area,'' or something similar to immediately indicate that you won't earn much salary, but the working conditions should be nice. If hired, you may not stay more than a year or two at that station, but you've just earned a year or two worth of commercial broadcasting facility experience.

Usually the ads urge prospective employees to ''Send tape and resume to. . . .'' and instead of the station's call letters and address there may be only a blind box number for the reply.

Newsman Gary Palay of Powell, Wyoming (chapter eight) found his first broadcasting job through a station's advertisement.

Aside from Help Wanted ads for radio and tv positions, many individual broadcasters will place Situation Wanted ads in an effort to be contacted by a potential employer. These brief classified ads will stress the individuals' accomplishments and strong desire to help a radio or tv station boost its ratings. Phrases such as ''highly motivated,'' ''solid references,'' and ''proven track record'' often are used in these ads.

The following is an alphabetized listing of major industry publications that regularly print classified job advertising. Costs for single issues and yearly subscriptions are included for your convenience. Some of these publications may be available at your local library's periodical or reference section, or you may be able to obtain a back issue from a local radio or television station.

ADVERTISING AGE
740 North Rush Street
Chicago, Illinois 60611
312-649-5200

Advertising Age, a well-read, weekly glossy newspaper, focuses on the many aspects of marketing. Most of the classified ads involve advertising agency or public relations company jobs; however, now and then an employer offers broadcast related positions such as scriptwriting or production work. Usually the employers here are seeking only experienced applicants.

Single copies are $1.50. Annual subscriptions are $57.

AMERICAN RADIO JOB MARKET
1553 North Eastern
Las Vegas, Nevada 89101

A weekly computerized listing of a hundred or more possible job opportunities, mostly in radio but some tv openings may be included. Single copies are $6 each or you can order six consecutive weekly mailings for $21.

BILLBOARD
1515 Broadway
New York, New York 10036
212-764-7300

The legendary tabulator that charts how well contemporary records are doing in sales and airplay across the country and around the world. The thick, colorful weekly magazine focuses on the music and home entertainment industries. Billboard is faithfully read by disc jockeys, and program and music directors.

You'll find only a few classified job ads and occasionally some ads for instructional courses or broadcasting schools.

Single copies are $3.50, a one-year subscription costs $148.

BROADCASTING
1735 DeSales Street N.W.
Washington, D.C. 20036
800-638-SUBS (toll-free subscription line)
202-638-1022 (main office phone number)

An excellent weekly magazine that is filled with news (geared to middle and upper management) about the radio, tv, cable, and communications satellite industries. The back of each issue usually contains a half dozen pages of classified help wanted and situations wanted advertising.

One up and coming young broadcaster I know found a job by spotting a news item elsewhere in Broadcasting magazine. In a weekly section devoted to ownership changes and stations changing formats, he noticed that one particular station had just been sold to a broadcast group known for strong, local news coverage. He correctly figured the new owners would beef up the news staff at their just acquired station. He applied for a job and was hired.

Single issues of Broadcasting magazine are $2 each, one-year subscriptions are $65.

BROADCASTING/CABLECASTING YEARBOOK

A superb, telephone-sized reference book that lists every radio and television station in the United States (and some foreign stations, too) by town, state, call letters, and programming format. Listings in this valuable volume also include the stations' addresses and phone numbers, and the names and titles of top station executives. Also included are similiar comprehensive listings for thousands of cable tv systems, broadcasting industry associations, equipment manufacturers, and programming services.

There are no job advertisements per se, but the yearbook is a wonderful source for job seekers. It does list about two dozen companies that provide employment and executive search services and there is a state-by-state listing of broadcasters' associations. Often these state associations have information about possible job openings in their region.

The *Broadcasting/Cablecasting Yearbook* is $85 per copy. Orders may be sent to the above address for Broadcasting magazine or may phoned in with the above toll-free number.

BROADCAST ENGINEERING
P. O. Box 12937
Overland Park, Kansas 66212-9981
913-888-4664

A monthly publication filled with information about state-of-the-art broadcasting equipment and techniques. The magazine is mailed free to "qualified persons" in the U.S. and Canada. The magazine defines "qualified" as anyone in "corporate management, engineers/technicians and other station management personnel at commercial and educational radio and tv stations. . . ."
Others may purchase a subscription for $25 a year. Single copies are available for $5 each. Broadcast Engineering usually contains one or two pages of classified help wanted ads for chief engineers and some entry-level engineering positions.

ELECTRONIC MEDIA
740 North Rush Street
Chicago, Illinois 60611
312-649-5200

A recent cousin to Advertising Age, Electronic Media also is published by the prolific Crain Communications, Inc. This well-written, glossy publication takes a thorough, weekly look at what is happening in all phases of the radio, tv, and cablecasting industries. You'll find a handful of help wanted classified ads.
Single issue price is 75 cents per copy, annual subscription price is $30.

MILLIMETER
P. O. Box 95759
Cleveland, Ohio 44101
212-477-4700 (New York editorial office)

This is the magazine of the motion picture and television production industries, geared to the technical end of the business. There are not many help wanted ads, but there are plenty of possible job leads because of the many other ads placed by industry companies promoting their goods and services.

Single issues are $5 each, one-year subscriptions cost $45.

RADIO & RECORDS
1930 Century Park West
Los Angeles, California 90067
213-553-4330

Known in the industry as "R&R," this weekly newspaper is filled with information from the radio and recording industries about who has been hired, fired, and promoted. Lots of information about new programming and equipment and lots of jobs are listed in the multi-page classified section.

Single copies cost $3.50, one-year subscriptions are $215; however, quarterly subscriptions also are available at only $60.

RTNDA JOB PLACEMENT SERVICE BULLETIN
1735 DeSales Street N.W.
Washington, D.C. 20036
818-883-6121 (Job placement information)
202-737-8657 (RTNDA main office)

A twice-monthly sheet with help wanted and situations wanted listings compiled by the Radio-Television News Directors Association. Jobs covered include news, weather and sports. Non-RTNDA members may purchase the bulletin at a cost of $8 for four issues. (No ads are taken by phone.)

TELEVISION/RADIO AGE
1270 Avenue of the Americas
New York, New York 10020
212-757-8400

Published every other week, Television/Radio Age is a well-produced magazine that looks in depth at issues and personalities in broadcasting and cable programming, management, marketing, and sales. Some classified job ads, but not many here.

Single issue price is $3.50 and one-year subscriptions cost $50.

19

WHAT YOU'LL GET PAID

*"Enough entry-level people
are competing for jobs
to keep most starting
salaries low."*

THE HUGE SALARIES paid to broadcasting Super Stars
create headlines, gossip, and delicious daydreams. If a major tv
network evening news anchor earns a million a year, surely
EVERYONE in broadcasting also must make big bucks, right?

Everyone who also is a major tv network evening news anchor
earns big bucks. But there are only a handful of these jobs and
they certainly are not entry-level positions. Even the high-paying
tv news anchor jobs at local stations in major markets are relatively
few compared to all the other news related jobs.

Whether it is in television or radio, entry-level jobs generally
do not pay much. In fact, the average starting salaries for broadcasting industry jobs did not increase from 1983 through 1985,
and they were consistently lower than the average starting salaries
in the advertising, newspaper, and public relations industries.

"Enough entry-level people are competing for jobs to keep most starting salaries low in broadcasting," explains Vernon A. Stone, chairman of the Southern Illinois University school of journalism who conducted a nationwide survey of broadcasting salaries for the Radio-Television News Directors Association. Professor Stone is the RTNDA's research director.

His survey of 450 television stations and 405 radio stations around the country indicated that most starting salaries in 1985 at smaller markets ranged from about $11,000 to $13,000 a year. That is less than some media Super Stars earn every WEEK.

A survey by the Dow Jones Newspaper Fund, Inc., of 3,160 journalism and communications graduates pegged the average 1985 radio and television starting salaries at around $11,000. That is the same dismal level as reported since 1983. The same survey showed that entry-level employees at daily newspapers and advertising agencies were paid about $13,500, and starting annual salaries at public relations companies were averaging about $14,500 in 1985.

On a happier note, the potential for heftier future paychecks apparently is much better in broadcasting. While starting salaries at small market radio and television stations may be only around $11,000, an aggressive, talented broadcaster lucky enough to jump from smaller to medium and larger markets may be able to boost his or her earnings in only a few years to $25,000 or more.

Mini-cam technicians in the top tv markets often work overtime and a few extra hours a day can push annual salaries into the $50,000 to $80,000 range.

Executive producers of major market tv newscasts can earn comparable wages. They, too, may work 12 hours a day.

A station sales representative who is good at making an eight percent commission selling radio or television spots at $4 or $40 each may be able to use those same selling skills to sign up sponsors in larger markets where the eight percent sales commission is based on commercial time that sells for $400 or $4,000 per minute.

Annual wages are not the only factor to contemplate, however. The actual cost-of-living also must be considered. A salary of $20,000 in Oklahoma City buys more bags of groceries than the same $20,000 in Los Angeles.

In 1980 I was very flattered to be offered an attractive broadcasting job in New York City with an immediate 35 percent salary increase. I politely turned down the job for personal reasons, but probably would have rejected it anyway because the wage increase would only cover the additional costs of living in the New York area and would not have resulted in any actual increase in my spending or savings power.

(Although by moving to New York I could have encountered the potential for an even higher salary in future years. When I moved from Kansas City to Chicago, my news writer's job paid roughly the same or even a bit less than the radio and television reporter's position I left behind in K.C. I gambled that while I would lose a bit of spending power with a higher cost of living in Chicago I would quickly get promoted to a higher salary. Besides, both my wife and I had relatives in Chicago and we figured we would not starve.)

The RTNDA study by Professor Stone shows there is not much salary difference between the lowest-paying jobs at small market and large market radio and tv stations. The range is roughly $11,000 to $15,600 for the lowest-paying staff positions.

On the other hand, there is a big difference between large and small markets in the reporters' and anchors' jobs. The range there is about $13,300 for a typical tv reporter's job in a small market to nearly $41,000 a year for a highly paid reporter in a top 25 market. In New York, Los Angeles, Chicago, Philadelphia, and other big cities, some reporters are paid well over $100,000 annually. And, the top news anchors can make considerably more.

Disc jockey salaries range from minimum wage in smaller markets to $100,000 and more annually for highly-rated, morning drive-time personalities with big audience ratings in big markets.

The following two charts will show the median weekly salaries for various radio and television industry jobs at stations across the country.

''ADI'' indicates ''Area of Dominant Influence.'' That's the fancy term for a station's geographical ''market,'' the size of the potential listenership or viewership in the station's primary broadcast signal area.

Professor Stone defines the radio market sizes this way:

Small Market—up to 50,000 potential listeners

Medium Market—50,000 to 250,000 potential listeners

Large Market—250,000 to a million potential listeners

Major Market—More than one million potential listeners

1985: Median Weekly Salaries in Radio News by Market

	Staff Low	Typical Reporter	High-paid Reporter	Typical Anchor	High-paid Anchor	News Director
Major Market	$299	$325	$400	$375	$526	$528
Large Market	$249	$251	$301	$258	$299	$351
Medium Market	$224	$232	$260	$249	$290	$300
Small Market	$200	$200	$223	$200	$225	$250

Definitions: A major-market station's broadcast could reach more than one million potential listeners; a large-market station's broadcast could reach 250,000 to one million potential listeners; a medium-market station's broadcast could reach 50,000 to 250,000 potential listeners; and a small-market station's broadcast could reach up to 50,000 potential listeners. The information is based on salary figures obtained from 405 radio news directors (representing 48 percent of the 850 commercial radio stations sent questionnaires) in response to a survey completed last month.

Information compiled by Professor Vernon A. Stone, head of the Journalism School, Southern Illinois University, Carbondale, IL. Chart reprinted by permission of The QUILL magazine.

1985: Median Weekly Salaries in TV News by Market

	Staff Low	Camera Operator	Typical Producer	High-paid Producer	Typical Reporter	High-paid Reporter	Typical Anchor	High-paid Anchor	News Director	Assignment Editor
ADI 1-25	$300	$538	$576	$680	$604	$786	$1,345	$2,500	$1,049	$675
ADI 26-50	$231	$366	$450	$570	$475	$576	$1,000	$1,633	$ 950	$518
ADI 51-100	$230	$288	$350	$400	$346	$425	$ 575	$ 844	$ 750	$450
ADI 101-150	$210	$240	$300	$312	$280	$335	$ 400	$ 525	$ 600	$365
ADI 151-212	$210	$225	$250	$330	$256	$300	$ 375	$ 451	$ 530	$338

ADI (Area of Dominant Influence) is TV jargon for the geographical area in which a television station's signal is considered dominant over competing signals from stations in other cities. The information is based on salary figures obtained from 450 television news directors (representing 60 percent of the 750 commercial TV stations listed in *Broadcasting Yearbook*) in response to a survey completed last month.

Information compiled by Professor Vernon A. Stone, head of the Journalism School, Southern Illinois University, Carbondale, IL. Chart reprinted by permission of The QUILL magazine.

20

NOW, A FEW LAST WORDS BEFORE WE SIGN OFF....

*"...relax...I will make
you a star...."*

HERE ARE SOME final thoughts you should consider as you prepare to launch your career in broadcasting. Some of these may seem like simple commonsense, but it doesn't hurt to emphasize them.

Pretend the studio microphones are ALWAYS on. Don't say anything around a radio or television studio that you would not want sent out over the airwaves. The "ON" light may be off, but the microphone still could be sending over the air everything that it picks up.

Everyone who has been in the industry for even a short period of time has experienced first hand the problems of saying or hearing something on an open microphone that was not supposed to go on the air. At the least the incident can be embarrassing, at worst it can mean instantly losing a job.

For decades the story has made the industry rounds about the children's tv program host who thought the camera and microphone were off at the end of the show when he told his studio crew (and the youngsters at home), "That should hold the little bastards for a while!"

The on-air studio microphones should always be considered "live," and "hot."

You may be so overwhelmed with joy about your first job in broadcasting that you probably won't become irritated with your boss for maybe a month. Eventually we all find problems with our jobs, that is just part of working, just part of life.

Here is some excellent advice a competent young man received a few years ago during a troubling period in his life. He passed it along to me as something to remember when frustrations get too big.

"Unless you own the station, it is not YOUR job. It is your employer's job and you are only filling it for them. The employer can do virtually anything he wants to with that job."

That puts an awful lot of frustration into perspective. I've now taken the attitude that unless my employer wants me to do something I honestly believe is illegal or against my moral standards, then I will do it. Sure, I will try to convince the Boss why we might be able to do something differently, do it my way; but the bottom line is this: My employer is paying me to do a job, and the employer has the right to expect that the job will be performed the way he or she wants it performed.

If more employees had this kind of attitude there might be less pettiness, less second-guessing, and less ulcers later in life.

Broadcasting can be a lot of fun (and filled with exciting challenges), but broadcasting is also a business. CBS sportscaster Brent Musburger used to tell his former Chicago colleagues, "I don't take myself seriously, but I do take my job seriously."

By the way, that young broadcaster who learned the lesson about employers' prerogatives and passed it along to me has moved up the industry ladder. He is now the General Manager of a major market educational tv station!

First impressions are indeed lasting impressions. When you show up for your first job interview (chapter three) even if you are auditioning for a job at a punk, heavy metal or acid rock music radio station, do not arrive resembling a member of the "Twisted Sister" rock group or anything similar.

There is much merit in the phrase "dress for success." You don't want to overdress, but a neat appearance certainly helps make a good impression. After you've established yourself in the business and people can judge you by a solid track record of achievements, then you can parade in public like Madonna or Boy George.

The old saying, "It's not what you know, but who you know," is not 100 percent correct in broadcasting, but close to it. If you don't know enough about your job to do it correctly, you may get fired or shuffled aside. Incompetence eventually may catch up to you. But to get your first job, it certainly helps to know as many people as possible in the industry.

And, then after you've met those people remember the advice of Personnel Director Karen Nance (chapter three):

"Don't burn your bridges. It sometimes is very difficult to avoid conflicts and confrontations with other employees, but avoid it if you can because you never know who you are going to be working for in the future.

"Can you imagine being a News Director and firing someone, then winding up two years later reporting to that person as your boss? It has happened in this industry."

And, the words of ABC News Editor Ron Gorski (chapter eight):

"...I didn't start working at ABC until five months after I got the job. Three days before I was supposed to start the new job there was a union strike at ABC. Fortunately, I wasn't yet officially part of ABC or the union, so I was able to stay at my old job in St. Louis on a freelance basis until the strike was over—but that took five months! It's a good thing I didn't burn any bridges at my previous job."

Finally, a few words about unions and agents.

If you work in a major market you may have to join a union. There are many unions representing off-air employees, writers, directors, and technical and engineering staff, and several unions that represent on-air talent, newscasters, disc jockeys and actors.

If you want to work in most states and the employer is a "union shop," then you pay the initiation fees and your regular union dues. Otherwise, you don't work there.

You may not have a choice about joining a union, but you certainly do have a choice about selecting an agent to represent you. Be careful. Real careful.

For entry-level jobs you probably do not need an agent. Job placement services can be helpful, but you probably don't need an agent to line up a personal services contract for your first job.

Many agents work hard on behalf of their clients, searching for jobs for them and assisting them in other ways such as legal work on contracts, financial planning and so on. But there are sharks in the water, too.

If you think you need an agent, shop around. Talk with others in the industry who have agents. What do they think about their current agent or others they've encountered?

Some agents may want a retainer fee for their services even before they do any work on your behalf. Others, following earlier standard procedures, take a fee only if they find work for you, and their fee is a previously determined percentage of the money you will be getting for that work.

Be careful of proposals to charge you a fee even if the agent fails to find a job that you take. You could face a large invoice for "professional services rendered" and not have any income because you still don't have a job.

Watch out, too, for agents who demand fees for job offers you received entirely on your own. Some agents will take "a cut" of all your media related activities whether or not they are responsible for getting them on your behalf.

Don't put your head too far in the clouds if your feet still are not touching the ground.

In 1976 I was approached by an attorney who still acts as an agent to some broadcasting industry performers. He wanted to get me hired as a television reporter or even an anchorman either in Chicago, Los Angeles, or Washington, D.C.

In my correspondence files I still have one of his letters dated April 23, 1976. The letter concludes: "I want you to relax, take it easy and I will make you a star yet."

I'm still waiting.

Index